Supercharged
GOOSEBUMPS 2481

JEREMY SMITH

Supercharged Goosebumps 2481

First published in Australia by Jeremy Smith 2019

Copyright © Jeremy Smith 2019
All Rights Reserved

 A catalogue record for this book is available from the National Library of Australia

ISBN: 978-0-6486617-0-2 (pbk)
ISBN: 978-0-6486617-1-9 (ebk)

Typesetting and design by Publicious Book Publishing
Published in collaboration with Publicious Book Publishing
www.publicious.com.au

No part of this book may be reproduced in any form, by photocopying or by any electronic or mechanical means, including information storage or retrieval systems, without permission in writing from both the copyright owner and the publisher of this book.

This book is dedicated to:

Mr John Alexander, Mr Jim Curtis,
Good Old 'Les' the smartest
truck driver ever,
and to my editor, Lesley Wyldbore

CONTENTS

CHAPTER 1:	SUFFERING IN SILENCE	1
CHAPTER 2:	RAW DEAL	7
CHAPTER 3:	ABUSED	12
CHAPTER 4:	HAM IN THE SANDWICH	19
CHAPTER 5:	RELIEF, REST AND RECOVERY	25
CHAPTER 6:	LOVE AT FIRST SIGHT	29
CHAPTER 7:	THE LONG HARD ROAD	33
CHAPTER 8:	POPPY SEEDS AND WATERMELONS	40
CHAPTER 9:	A WILD AND ROUGH RIDE	46
CHAPTER 10:	THE FIGHT OF MY LIFE	63
CHAPTER 11:	THE SCOTTISH GENTLEMAN	68
CHAPTER 12:	KICKED WHILE YOU'RE DOWN	72
CHAPTER 13:	PROFESSIONAL ERROR OF JUDGEMENT	81
CHAPTER 14:	I CAN SEE THE CHEQUERED FLAG	173
CHAPTER 15:	THE LAST LAUGH	179

1

SUFFERING IN SILENCE

30 November 2014
Greystanes, Sydney, Australia

I was born 25 July 1971 at the Parramatta Hospital, Sydney, NSW.

Growing up here as a little boy was a time I will never forget. Especially the values and love I was shown by Aunty Betty, Uncle Bruce, and the Townsends (Phillip, Peter and Paul), our never to be forgotten neighbours.

This is where my love for cars and motorbikes was first initiated and developed and all boys 15+ years older than me shared the same love and passion as I. The first time I sat on a big high-powered motorbike was at the tender age of only two, which I remember as if it were yesterday. The roar of those engines is just something I fell head over heels in love with. It was the same with the many cars that the Townsends purchased over the years. I remember vividly the night when my mother, father, two sisters and I drove into the driveway of our Bolaro Avenue property, and the exhaust system fell off on the driveway, WOW! That was one of the best sounds I had ever heard, our green XB Falcon sounded like a real race car. We were driving a car like the Gadgen brothers, strong family friends of the Townsends with whom I shared many photos and TV clips of them racing with Uncle Bruce. The Gadgen brothers were also associated with race car driver Allan Moffatt – who shared a Bathurst win in 1973 – as well as race car driver Kevin Bartlett too.

Sadly, as we only found out this last 10–12 years ago, my eldest sibling endured a horrifying time in her life where she was severely abused at the age of only ten; this was when for me the beatings began. I was only 4 ½ years old when she turned from caring to overly abusive, most of which went undetected by our parents. Things from here on would always be strange and awkward between her and I.

One thing I clearly remember was that my mum and Aunty Betty loved to shop at Parramatta shopping mall, better known now as Westfield shopping centre, Parramatta. My mum enjoyed her part time job at Target.

February–March 1977

We moved to Byron Bay in NSW in early 1977, where we resided with my father's parents, Frederick Stanley and Delma Joyce Smith. I would forever miss Aunty Betty, Uncle Bruce, Philip, Pete and Paul. Here I would really look up to my pop and giggle at my nana the way she started to call my pop a "Pommy Prick"; this became a regular occurrence. As I write this, I am now covered from head to foot in goosebumps and very teary-eyed. This is where my life took a really nasty turn as I found myself before reaching the age of seven being sexually abused by my paternal grandfather almost every day for approximately 16–18 months. As a little boy I just believed this was a normal way of life and part of growing up. It was here that I was given a purebred collie dog for my 7th birthday who would become my best mate. The beatings from my eldest sister started again, but I was too little to understand why this was happening again and why more often – a lot of the time several times daily. She would beat me in front of the fireplace endlessly with a cast iron fire stoke, mainly to the back and side of the skull. I thought she was going to kill me. I was confused as to why there was so much aggression; some days she was happy and caring and other days completely angry, abusive and erratic. Most of what would happen to me, happened at night in the black forests of the

Jeremy Smith

Everglades, Byron Bay, NSW, now known as Byron at Byron Resort & Spa, Byron Bay NSW 2481. I became indescribably afraid of the dark until I was around 22–23 years' old. While this horrifying event was taking place, I would wet the bed 2–5 times a night on most days of the week. One would think that normal parents would question what was going on, but in those days children were to be seen and most certainly not heard. Speaking up would have been absolutely pointless as you would be punished; that's why children of our era didn't dare bother, because you would be crucified if you did.

19 April 2015

I went on leading a very happy life as best I could, but always wondering and constantly asking myself questions even at this young age of around seven. I would soon be caught with a cousin in the mower shed involving sexual activity which at the time I thought was perfectly normal. I carried on looking up to my pop but always somewhat confused and at times completely puzzled. I must say the things I loved most were my two dogs Rocky and Lassie and those sounds of our three-wheeler mini bikes, the old grey tractor and the infamous green field ride on the lawnmower and my Road King 3-speed metallic blue pushbike doing skids and pedalling burnouts wherever I could. I started to enjoy the music of

ABBA and slowly began to relate to it. I would pursue an education at Byron Bay Primary School firstly under the teaching of Miss Lorraine Atwell, Principal John Alexander, Deputy Principal Neil Duncan and other teachers such as Ken and Sue Thurlow, Sally Stead, Julie McCellan, Karen Peak, Mrs Finch and many more. Here I constantly received on the bottom of my school reports, "Does he ever stop talking?" That was my way of finding out things for myself and still is even now at 43 years of age. At this school I underwent beatings almost straight away from the same five boys. This gradually, but also fairly quickly, developed into a daily event, where finally at about age 8 ½ – 9, the doctors took me out of school for a period of about 3 ½ months, where I would live on grated apple and water only. Doctors' orders were strictly 'no school' and why I had the most enlarged liver they had ever seen on a child of this age was put down as a medical mystery, with no real reason medically as to why? The 'WHY' was being bashed and kicked in the stomach continuously by these same five boys. I would say nothing as I was sworn to secrecy for the very real fear of things getting much worse.

I engaged in sprinting, soccer and Nippers[1] at an early age. I started running at approximately the age of six, soccer at 7 ½ and Nippers at nine, and eventually surfing seven days a week too. I could never do enough sport. I was scared of the water due to two very different near drownings. One at age four years in an old well in a nursery somewhere in Sydney; and another time at Cronulla beach in Sydney at a Nippers[1] country titles event at the age of ten where, although the beach was closed by the local authorities, the dads still let us go out purely because it was our thing. With an approximate 8–10 ft swell this would be the end for me of swimming in pools and never to enter the water at the beach. I became terrified of the water, at least for now.

My mates would now start to develop; Jason Gilmore, Dave Williams, Adam Woolridge, Brad (Clava) Pullen, David (Frank) Schipp, Jason (Chucky) Rutter, Greg and Mike McCabe, Craig Cornish, Todd (Batto) Batson, Robbie (Marrsy) Marr, Gavin (Big Gav) Nichols, Michael Clark, Shaun O'Neil, Mark Alexander, Robert (Blummo) Blumson and many, many more, too many to list.

---

1. Australian-based surf lifesaving competition.

2

RAW DEAL

I would now start to take on Nippers and soccer pretty seriously. I joined Nippers under 9's at a late age. As a previous sprinter I quickly and successfully engaged in being a serious competitor in Nippers, mainly on the sand because of my fear of the water. It never really registered with me back then how much of a will I had to win, how I really *wanted* to win, second was not an option. I became national champion at beach sprinting twice and national champion at beach flags two or three times too. We also had an undefeated beach relay team which won the national championships three times consecutively. My main rivals, which caused me time and time again millions of stomach butterflies were Michael Clark (Byron Bay) Peter Young (Ballina) Shaun O'Neil (Byron Bay) and eventually Michael Player of Kingscliff NSW. I was eventually pushed and persuaded to undertake water activities in the pools and the ocean. I also eventually went on to win swimming, board paddle and eventually the iron man but only at club and branch level, never anything higher. I went on to be the most successful and highest point-scoring Nipper ever in the history of the Byron Bay Surf Club, even better than Thomas Clunie, someone I completely idolised my entire surf club years. He only knew how to win, not how to come second, third or fourth. He would be my most respected 'Nipper' and I believe the best ever "Nipper of the Year" in the history of the Byron Bay Surf Club to date. The following year came the time when I was told by certain officials that I was the highest ever point-scorer as a Nipper in the history of the Byron Bay Surf Club and was set to achieve "Nipper of the Year". WOW! Equivalent to Thomas Clunie! I didn't think this was possible as to me, he was the best. To be classed as the same as him was unbelievable and unthinkable as well as a serious privilege and honour.

We sat there on the grass in front of the surf club, as we had done all the other years, waiting for the announcement of "Nipper of the Year", and the announcer paused and hesitated. He then went on to say that this year they had changed the nipper of the year to the most improved nipper of the year and 'this year the award goes to … Mike McCabe'. My heart dropped to my feet and my goosebumps disappeared 1,000 times quicker than they turned up. This was thanks very much to none other than the infamous town arsehole Mr Clark. One of the town's most two-faced arseholes and one of the biggest pigs I had ever met on this planet. Other than this, years 9, 10, 11, 12 and 13 of my life would most probably be the best between my love of soccer and Nippers apart from the "Nipper of the Year" devastation which I would never really get over. I have carried the disappointment and the hurt with me my entire adult life.

30 April 2015

I must mention that the near drowning at age 10–10 ½ I remember ever so vividly; I was on my last breath stuck in a massive gutter with no way out and was preparing to die with immense fear very quickly. As I began to give up, completely exhausted and three-quarters full of water, miraculously out of nowhere my primary school principal John Alexander saved my life, way ahead of the two qualified lifesavers from the home club. He saved my life only in his socks and jocks and a quick grab of a lifesaver's rescue board. I would be forever grateful, and later in life found myself on several occasions in a position to thank him, but I just never knew how to. So, Mr "A" here is a lifetime of thanks from me, I will be forever grateful, and I will never forget that I owe my life to you.

Later, in my teenage years, Mr "A" would lose his beautiful wife – much loved by her family and the whole town where she was a local hospital sister and very well respected by all – to a horrifying terminal illness. Throughout my life I would never forget Mr and Mrs "A" and their two sons, Peter and Mark.

At the age of approximately 11 my father became a local Byron Bay councillor and began life as a local developer in the region of Suffolk Park. He would only last a few years. He tried to develop approximately 25–30 acres of beachfront land and was constantly bullied and harassed by other council colleagues owing to several bouts of major corruption. He quickly failed and ended up in financial ruin. This would be the beginning of years of heartache for mostly my mum and I, being the only son. He crucified everyone closest to him for his failure, except for the only person who really deserved it, of course no other than himself. Life would be misery under our roof for many years to come after this event of failure. I would push on with life and put my focus on girls, sport and lots of driving and riding motorbikes and I started looking at joining the workforce full-time at the youthful age of 15 and with only the completion of year 10 in education at Mullumbimby High School in northern NSW.

Me and one of my best mates Brad Pullen (Clava) gained access to his stepdad's (Don Baker) motorbikes. We went for a casual ride on the bikes up to Coopers Shoot, Byron Bay, where we came across a nice stretch of straight road; it was here that I gave him the nod, the green light was only seconds away, the race was on. We got to a top speed of only 140km/hr, but I came off at 120km/hr at only 14 years of age, entering a right hander only to lock the front brake with a bald tyre. Doing somersaults at 120km/hr beside the bike was something I would never forget. I loved it, I pulled up on my arse one metre short of a barbed wire fence and a boulder twice the size of me. I removed hundreds of thistles from my hands for weeks to come. Clava's response was "Fuck, is the bike alright?" I said, "You miserable bastard, I just flirted with death, and all you are worried about is the bike." "Sorry mate!" he said. "Are you alright?" "I'm fine, just a little sore and my arms and hands are full of these fucking thistles." A lifetime memory and laughter would forever come from this event.

3

ABUSED

To escape the dark days of my childhood I now focused my mind 100% on work. I became an indentured apprentice as a pastry cook at the Byron Bay Hot Bread Kitchen, where I began to enjoy and learn as much as I possibly could about pastry and cake production. I worked very long hours, no less than 55–60 hours per week, and that was when the business was quiet. Up to 65–75 hours when we were flat strap. Earning an income of my own was a very satisfying thing. Then, just as everything started falling into place for me at around 16 ½ years of age, I was transferred from the Byron Bay shop to a new retail outlet in the suburb of Suffolk Park. Here I worked no less than 14 and up to 18 hours per day. This became a very regular routine. I was working for a very troubled chronic alcoholic gambler and this turned out to be yet another frightening ordeal for me. I started to think that every apprentice would be treated like this and, just as I did when I was 6 ½ years old, I simply thought this was a normal way of life. My father would drive me to work at 11:45 p.m. every night, five days a week and in my second year of apprenticeship, I would cry almost every night begging him to do something about my work situation and its conditions. His reply was always "No, and if you don't want to continue in your job, you will be going straight back to school instantly". I became scared on a daily basis, working one on one with my indentured boss. I wet myself constantly, multiple times a day, because I wasn't allowed to go to the toilet as he became increasingly aggressive and would scream at me if I did, as he deemed it a waste of time. But let me tell you this, when someone throws knives, palette knives and three-strap bread tins at you with force, you become so nervous and shit scared, you want to wee every 10–15 minutes. I just became so scared. I found it incredibly embarrassing, but easier just to wet myself, and this went on for approximately 14 months. I can remember clearly about 3.30 one morning when he turned up to work, drunk as usual and started on me. Finally, I found the emotional strength to defend myself and I fucking exploded, this was the beginning for me to start standing up for myself in life. The constant abuse changed me from a soft-natured person, into a very tough, no bullshit type of young teenager. One would have thought and hoped that my father would stand up for me, but there was no such possibility. From this day on I realised that my biological father was nothing but a coward and that I would never understand. While I was in a rage with my employer I rang his dad immediately at the Byron Bay shop and quickly proceeded to tell him that if I didn't go back into the town shop I would resign at the end of the week; my request was granted with immediate effect.

26 June 2015

I looked forward to going back to the town shop and working with a team, not just one on one like the Suffolk Park site, with a boss that was supposed to start with me at 11.30 p.m. but would only eventually show up between 3–3.30 a.m., leaving me there alone for 3–4 hours and think nothing of it even though I was just a young kid.

My passion and love for cars and motorbikes began to escalate quickly as I started to slowly earn and save money. There were three brothers and one daughter in the family I worked for. One of the brothers, Doug, is a person I will never forget; he treated me like his own little brother, he had a big heart and was a very generous bloke, a good, no bullshit human being who took crap from nobody, especially his brothers. The father, Les, had a heavy interest in owning racehorses and gambling heavily on them. I took an interest in this and would soon end up a chronic gambler myself. In many more ways than one I would use gambling as a coping mechanism to escape the many demons in my life so far at the young age of only 16 ½ years old.

I always loved my sport in all and many different forms; I became a massive Mick Doohan fan and ultimately just as big a fan of Mark (Skaiffey) Skaiffe, Craig Lowndes, Dick Johnson and Peter Brock. I would set my alarm clock at weird and wonderful hours just to see Mick Doohan race, and always fingers crossed for him to win, the world's best natural born motorcyclist champion and a true blue down to earth top bloke, the same with Skaiffey and Lowndes, Johnson and Brock. That's when you are really proud to be an Aussie, when you are represented by characters like this.

24 July 2015

Touching just 17 things became increasingly more scary and violent for me as the youngest son of the family by whom I was employed beat me up several times. Many times, if I saw him in the vicinity of the Hot Bread Kitchen fuelled up on alcohol, I would lock the back doors as quickly as I could, always in fear of my life. He would assault me in the pitch-black dark of the laneway behind the shop, always hiding beside the toilet waiting for me to appear. As I mentioned earlier this was also a major contributing factor of me being shit scared of the dark until 22–23 years old. One night clearly and deeply stamped within my brain was the night I let him in when he presented me with a plate-size fish and demanded that I make him a fish pie. I told him that I couldn't as I didn't know how to. He then instantly became extremely agitated and began to slap me aggressively in the face with the fish, and eventually ended up beating me with the fish and his fist. He beat my head with the fish positioned over several places of my face and continuously beat into the fish with his fist. I tried to get away from him, but this only made matters ten times worse, so I just copped it and hoped and prayed that I would stay alive. Eventually he left the fish almost non-existent, and me in an incredible mess covered in fresh flesh, with another incredible mess in the kitchen to clean up. I breathed a sigh of relief, completely shattered with emotion and extreme fear that he would come back. I cleaned myself up with warm soapy water and cleaned up the mess on the benches and all over the floor, but washing the fish out of my hair was going to be tricky.

The other three staff, including his father, would arrive at midnight to start work, I didn't dare say a word to anyone ever, always fearing for the future of my life. He went on to become very well known to every police force across Australia and ended up spending time in watch houses[2] constantly as time went by. The only human being on the planet who had the slightest idea of what I endured is a very close lifelong mate of mine, Simon Curtis. He also started an apprenticeship with the same people and would also have a pretty tough life with constant abuse and the slave-driven type labour we were forced to engage in week after week, but for me with no support from home, leaving was not an option because I didn't want to re-engage in school 18–24 months behind, with all my friends approaching the end of year 12.

I would try as much as possible to block out the traumatic work life with my love of cars and motorbikes and now, fairly seriously, girls. Driving fast and riding fast on my bikes momentarily took my mind off the constant abuse. I truly believe this was what kept me going; now that I look back, I actually don't know how I kept going, and don't know anyone that could, but like I said quitting wasn't an option. I know for a fact that after all the constant abuse and

---

2. Local police station-based jail cells.

Jeremy Smith

traumatic times one after the other this would turn me into an incredibly high-risk daredevil type character. I constantly told myself things would get better and took on board people saying things in conversation like "life wasn't meant to be this hard" and "life is a gamble". I always wondered whether other human beings were having trouble like this or if my experiences were extreme.

4

HAM IN THE SANDWICH

26 August 2015

From 14–17 years old, me and my mates would experience an awkward amount of unlicensed driving and motorbike riding. Mostly me behind the wheel, Friday and Saturday nights, Byron to Ballina at 100 mph, something I loved then and still do now, it's in my blood. Clava and I would continue our road trips and racing on Don Baker's motorbikes, sensational fun but strongly not advised by me to today's youth, things have seriously changed. Eventually things caught up with me one Saturday night when Dave Williams and I were caught in the Pacific Vista Estate by two police officers from the Byron Bay station. Unlicensed sort of, only one of us with a worker's permit licence[3] due to age[4]. The coppers threw the

---
3. Licence provided to an underage rider/driver for commuting to work.
4. I received my working licence at 15-years-old.

book at us. Me for being unlicensed out of working hours with an illegal pillion passenger on the back, no 'L' plate (a total of three fines), and Dave a fine for being an unlawful pillion passenger. We didn't even know what a pillion passenger was, but we quickly figured out it was the poor bastard on the back. We laughed it off after a week or so and got on with life, AUD$185 later. Many thanks to copper Millsy I never lost my licence and the charges were somewhat relaxed as he was officer in charge that night.

The second two years of my apprenticeship became increasingly awkward as the family of Leo and Marcia Rooke and sons Brett and Darren joined forces in a partnership with the family that I worked for. This was a disaster from the get-go. The two families despised one another from about the first three months in. Leo would often say to me "I detest that family and I regret ever selling my business in Sydney and moving to Byron Bay".

I quickly became a pawn, not so much from the Rookes' side but most definitely from the other family's side. They began to use me as a scapegoat, bouncing me from one family to the other, saying that I had done this and that, and that I had said this and that, but every single bit of it was bullshit and lies time after time. Just one person covering up for another and blaming me, an easy target, just a young

18-year-old kid. Until the Rookes joined forces with the family I worked for, we always endured a 39-hour 2-day shift over Easter. Thursday night, 21 hours, backed up by an 18-hour shift on the Friday night. I remember clearly having only 4 ½ –5 hours for a shit, shave and shower, not to mention sleep or a spare second to yourself. I would ride my push bike home at the end of shift every year, delirious and dizzy with a feeling of drunkenness, wanting to throw up from just sheer exhaustion. But, ask my good mate Simon Curtis and he will tell you.

26 August 2015

As I said we worked 39 hours in only two days with the rest of the week still to complete. We would be rewarded with 20 dollars, cash in hand and a dozen hot cross buns. What a generous pack of miserable fucken arseholes they were. As much money as they could possibly make to put on those racehorses that they owned. What parents would allow this to happen? I know I most certainly would not.

At 19 I had enough equity from my first two cars, both Toyota Corollas. I eventually upgraded to an SX-100 Toyota Corolla, known back then as the V8 chaser. This car would become my pride and joy, as all I did was work and sleep and when there was enough time and energy I loved to surf. Never too much more than that. I paid AUD $25,000 on the road[5] for this car when I was 19. It would be treated no differently than a newborn baby. I had owned the vehicle for no more than three weeks when the arsehole, who had already assaulted me several times, poured flavoured milk and cream all over my brand-new car. Obviously, it seeped down into the doors and eventually went sour and stayed rotten for many months after. I would have loved to be able to flog him, but this was impossible at the time. Stupid me, I sold him the flavoured milk, cream and even the meat pie that was also smeared all over the paint work. I found it some 10–11 hours later at the end of shift. A very jealous and deranged fucking arsehole, who wasn't capable of finding full-time employment. These beatings and constant abuse, both physical and verbal, would trouble me throughout my entire adult life. One thing I did know for sure was that it would force me to be an incredibly mentally tough human being. I would end up fearing no one and nothing. I would, however, end up with an incredibly wild temper, something I must say I am not proud of, but in some sad way it was forced upon me through little or no support from my family. I would be psychologically scarred for life.

---

5. All govt charges/stamp duties, etc. and registered.

As all I did was work and had nothing really to spend my money on, my cars were predominately my main pride and joy. Motorbikes came a close second. But there is simply nothing more soul destroying than when your father tells you, "If you bring that $25,000 car home to my house you will not be permitted to sleep under my roof".

15 December 2015

The truth being 'Hot Shot' Rex Smith 'The Failed Developer' didn't want to see his son driving a car far superior to his. A $1,000 XD Falcon shitbox full of rust that never started without major persistence. This was the result of his repossessed wank mobile, a Volvo 244 GLE – we all know about Volvo drivers, right? Well he fit the image well and truly, say no more.

Finally, the day came, 17 January 1991, when my apprenticeship would finally and assuredly expire, I was now qualified and certified as a pastry cook with proficiency. I resigned with immediate effect. Freedom at last. I was soon to take up employment with Sunny Brand Chickens near Byron Bay industrial estate and was very grateful for the start as I was unemployed.

The day I resigned to eventually leave the bakery, Leo Rooke begged me to stay. I simply said "Leo I have had

Jeremy Smith

four years of this fucking shit! Used, abused and ripped off, you have only had two years of it". He still pleaded with me and begged me to stay, right up until I got into my car and strapped on the seatbelt. I replied "Leo, thanks but no thanks, I have had a complete gutful of this fuckin' crap".

5

RELIEF, REST AND RECOVERY

23 June 2016

I worked for only six months as a factory worker and I must say with a fantastic group of people, including all staff, management and the two partner/owners Sam Gilmore and Ron Lang; to be honest compared to handcrafting food, I found it incredibly boring but was completely grateful for the start and income. Thanks a lot Sammy. At the 5 ½ month mark one of the office staff called me from the factory floor to tell me that there was a man here to see me. 'Who the fuck could this be?' I said to myself. I walked out of the factory and there stood the man himself, Leo Rooke, a boss for whom I had gained a significant amount of respect. He asked me how I was and if I was happy here and whether I would consider coming back as they had been through five or six different blokes who had filled my position in the last six months. Leo said that no one was prepared to put up with the working conditions, let alone the miserable amount of money they were paid. "I wonder why," I said. "So, nothing has changed, why the fuck would I ever come back?" was my response to Leo. He replied that it had changed as of yesterday, so I asked, "What the hell has changed?" Leo said, "I went to Industrial Relations in Lismore yesterday and reported my business partners for extremely underpaying all of their employees". I just laughed and said, "Well fuck me, that is the best thing I have heard in nearly five years". "Okay Leo," I said, "what's the deal?" He told me that I would be paid for every hour I work from the moment I start, that is, if I accept. "When do you want me to start Leo?" I asked. He replied, "I know this is extremely short notice, but tomorrow night at midnight, we are in the deepest shit we have ever been in". I had about 30 seconds to give him an answer as I had to get back to the factory to work, and I felt bad about not being able to give the chicken farm the appropriate notice, but I didn't have much of a choice. With a very firm handshake I said, "Leo, see you tomorrow night at midnight". With a very big smile he said, "Mate, I am truly grateful, and I won't let you down". "I know," I said, "that's why I am coming back". He turned and walked away; we were both happy with the deal we had just made.

Supercharged Goosebumps 2481

24 June 2016

The next 18 months were the most enjoyable time for me in my job at the Hot Bread Kitchen. The amazing difference of being paid for 20+ hours of overtime would make things so much more rewarding and a shitload more stress free. It was amazing how quickly the hours of work had reduced from 60+ hours a week back to a maximum of 50 hours per week. It truly was fucking laughable. Purely a one-way street, greed like I had never seen in my life before and haven't ever since to date.

2 August 2016

The year of 1992 would probably be the most memorable year of my life. I had my 21st birthday party at the Byron Bay Surf Club with family and my closest friends, who were so many great people. Those photos of our Nipper days on the surf club walls would forever make me feel somewhat unsettled. We had a sensational night of partying and much to the disgust of my parents – the square pants sponge bobs that they were – they learned of all my unlicensed driving and motorbiking over many years. One might say not that hard to outsmart. The look on their faces was priceless. "Our son doing these kinds of illegal practices, it just couldn't be true," they said. I guess I would say they were trying to raise a 3rd daughter not a son.

In August 1992, I finally resigned from my job once and for all, never to return, what a fucking relief that was. A seriously huge weight lifted off my shoulders.

6

LOVE AT FIRST SIGHT

The Friday night before my 21st, I was at the Beach Hotel in the corner playing the card machines with a group of my mates, when I spotted a blonde bombshell out of the corner of my eye. I quickly introduced myself and she told me her name was Vanessa Jane Hogan. A night that I would never forget; it would be stamped firmly on my brain forever as probably the best moment of my life by far. Finally, I would have something and someone to help me move on from Byron Bay indefinitely and permanently. I would never ever look back. I was so extremely happy to see Byron Bay in my rear-view mirror for the final time. But I must make it clear, I would forever miss those beaches. The best in Australia without a doubt.

I took up residency on the Gold Coast in October 1992 and landed the best job – still to date – that I ever had. I was employed as a junior pastry chef in the kitchens of the Conrad

Jupiters Hotel and Casino – now known as The Star Gold Coast. I was 21 ½ and reported to Executive Chef Gunther Karch and Assistant Executive Pastry Chef Hubert Veh. I was so grateful to be given the opportunity to work in such a state-of-the-art kitchen environment and with some of the world's best people in the culinary industry. I was quickly promoted to three higher positions in just three years.

My relationship with Vanessa blossomed quickly and started to really shine. Finally, there were some awesome positives coming at me left, right and centre. Leaving Byron Bay would be the greatest thing I ever experienced. With incredibly mixed emotions and feelings and memories never to be forgotten – the wicked experiences I had endured at such a tender age had scarred my brain and my heart for life. With absolutely no support from my so-called father, those scars would grow deeper and stronger as I grew older and began to realise that life wasn't as gruelling as I had so far experienced it to be.

26 September 2016

In December 1992, I met two of the most fantastic blokes I have ever been involved with, Martin Reisch, a German pastry chef, and Serdar Yener, a Turkish born executive pastry chef. I looked up to Martin as the older brother I always wished

I'd had, and most definitely I looked to Serdar Yener – better known as "Yener" – as the father figure in my life that I had never really had either. The only fathering I had experienced was abusive, extremely negative and most of the time humiliating. Being raised by a man who was so pessimistic would most certainly take its toll on me. I tried again and again to be extremely optimistic and as positive as I could, but constantly being brought down by a failed pessimistic developer was a lifelong heartache for me to live with as his so-called son. Martin and Yener supported me in a way that I had never been able to imagine. They turned me into the best pastry chef I could possibly be through huge amounts of love, honesty and – most importantly – something that I had never been shown, respect. That automatically brings the excellence out in any human being. It provides you with a massive amount of self-worth.

Coming home from a job that I loved to a woman that I loved even more, was a dream come true, something that money couldn't buy. I worked with some of the most awesome people, both guys and girls, at the Conrad Jupiters, and have sensational memories I will hold close to my heart for the rest of my life. This was for me, an experience of a lifetime after coming from a past working life in Bryon Bay that I could explain as nothing other than sheer misery. The four-year stint at the Conrad Jupiters prepared me for a great adult working life, something that I would strongly advise everyone in the culinary world to try and experience.

In 1994 Vanessa and I bought our first house on Roundelay Drive, Stephens, better known now as Varsity Lakes QLD. We were there for approximately four months when we were given our first child, a four legged, four-month-old beautiful furry friend by the name of Zac. He was an abused RSPCA puppy who quickly ended up being my best mate and we took him everywhere with us. He was the most unbelievable animal you could ever wish for, smart, loving and incredibly loyal.

The Conrad Jupiters working life came to an end in late October 1996, when at 25 years old I was offered a management role with Woolworths Ltd as one of their 'Fresh Food Department Managers'. This job would be short-lived as I derived absolutely no job satisfaction here, apart from some of the great people I worked with every day; Robyn, Flo, Bob, Nick, Kevin and my immediate staff in the bakery department. I stayed exactly 12 months to the day purely for CV reasons only.

7

THE LONG HARD ROAD

26 September 2016

On 6 October 1997 we took ownership of our first little cake shop/bakery in Mermaid Waters on the Gold Coast. As life went on, I increasingly had the desire to go faster and faster in every form of the word, especially work. Although I was told every day of my apprenticeship that I was way too slow, I had now discovered that this was nothing but slave driving talk. Over the years, because I had worked with hundreds of other pastry cooks and chefs, I soon learned that I was by far one of the quickest. My need to produce beautiful food for people to enjoy grew more passionate – thanks to Martin and Yener – as did my love for fast cars and motorbikes.

We began our hard slog as small business owners thanks to a loan of AUD$25,000 from my Uncle Bill and Aunty Lyn.

Jeremy Smith

The business wasn't even turning over $3,000 per week when we bought the business, but in our first week turnover was a staggering $5,800 for no reason other than a super clean environment and simply super fresh good food. Not rocket science, just working off a refined "KISS" principle. Yep, for those of you who don't know, it means "Keep It Simple Stupid". The theory normally works well until some clown tries to complicate it, and that goes for every and any industry. And the old 80/20 principle works whatever business you apply it to: 80% of sales come from 20% of the customers. Just ask the likes of Coca Cola and Carlton United Breweries. The 80/20 principle also applies to most forms of generalised life as well, people with university degrees and people with trade-based skills as well as just plain everyday human beings.

    The first six months was mainly me and my good mate Stewy Pontin. We worked no less than 115 hours per week, 7 days a week, and fuck me, we worked. Stewy was a chef by trade with a Swiss certification in pastry as well. He was a sensational help in getting this little business off the ground. I know I nearly killed you Stewy, but hey, we both lived to tell the tale. Thanks a lot mate, gratefully appreciated by Vanessa and I, we couldn't have done it without you. On the counter were Vanessa, Sandra and Rhonda. Sadly, this little business topped out at $6,800 per week, and with a horrendous rent of $960 per week – don't forget this was back in 1997 – that was a lot of bread, cakes and pastries to make before you made a dollar for yourself. We had a Chinese landlord by the name of Mr Yung. This bloke ripped several fellow tradesmen in the Newcastle/Maitland area through works done from the earthquakes that took place in the 1990s for which contractors weren't paid, and yep, you guessed, it he just happened to be our Gold Coast landlord at our small business located in Mermaid Waters QLD. We had four very enjoyable and memorable years here in this strip shopping centre, but the fifth year became our biggest ever nightmare. Eventually there would be a complete shop shuffle at this shopping centre.

All of the Australian tenants would slowly and surely be forced or pushed out, leaving many of them in financial ruin, with the news agency, pizzeria and ourselves as the only Aussies still trading, but all eventually completely 100% replaced by Chinese and Vietnamese shops, including ours. But I must say the memories from here will always be bright and vivid as I met some of the greatest human beings I have ever met including the Hackett and Wingrave families, my personal solicitor who replaced the retired Kevin Copley, a bloke by the name of Matthew Busby – and wasn't he a funny bastard, a real true blue – Clive Anthony from whom I learnt loads of business knowledge and he should know because he was the real deal and wasn't he savage at retail business, he seriously was one of the best in the business to date for me and I had the utmost respect for him. I also became a massive fan of our Australian swimming great Grant Hackett and wasn't he just a sensational human being. I also met hundreds and hundreds of great local people within the Mermaid area in my 10 years of business and I was truly grateful for that.

One day after a 12-month period of constant threats and several bouts of major intimidation and harassment with some involvement from my solicitor at the time Kevin Copely, I drove into the centre one Sunday afternoon and saw red when I spotted Mr Yung in his fruit and vegetable shop. I went straight for the jugular, grabbed him by the throat and said, "Please just answer one question for me. When you were 30 years of age did you have a fuckhead like yourself trying to get in your way of making a living for you, your wife and your four children?" He wouldn't answer so I squeezed a little harder on his throat and I screamed, "Answer my fucking question!" And as his eyeballs turned to the size of snooker balls he quickly answered, "No I did not!" I let him go immediately so he could catch a little oxygen and help those eyeballs return to marble-like size. He was exhausted, and I said to him nose to nose, "You will always beat me with your chequebook, but you'll never beat me with your brawn, because you don't have any, you scrawny little Chinese cunt." I then gently whispered in his ear, "If you cause me any more trouble, I will kill you, you prick, I will tear your throat out with my fist. Oh and by the way Hong, I don't make promises to anyone but this is my promise to you, whatever you do don't ever walk in front of me when I am driving a motor car, I will run you over and do a reverse burnout on top of you and splatter you all over your own shopping centre wall and to be quite honest that's how all of your tenants would love to remember you by. Your own signature all over your own commercial property wall."

The constant threats and tireless harassment ceased immediately. This arsehole would never play games or fuck with me or my family ever again. But I was forced to sell to the Vietnamese. This was a strict condition of being granted a lease as we didn't have one and this was highly illegal. We eventually sold the shop and thankfully got the hell out of there. In among this above-mentioned shit fight we opened a second outlet at Mermaid Beach on the Gold Coast Highway. I ran the two businesses with between 18–26 staff depending on the season. This only lasted for approximately 20 months thank goodness; it was a financial nightmare and a constant migraine pretty much 24/7, well at least for the time that I was awake, which was approximately 135 hours per week.

I applied for an immediate sponsorship from Panadeine

Forte[6] and sponsorship was granted. I wish! We endured an approximate capital loss of about AUD$30–35,000 in round figures, eventually I stopped counting. In among this we would also weather cash theft from our staff, with a loss of approximately AUD$135,000 over a short period of only 20 months as my then wife had birthed our first two children and was unable to help with the business. Yes, it sounds like a substantial amount of money and yes, indeed it was for such a small business, but the return on stock investment was so out of whack it wasn't funny, we were being robbed blind. It was almost impossible to catch as it equated to an approximate AUD$125–135 per day per shop, but it was pretty near impossible to pay rent and wages, let alone stock and some drawings for ourselves, which was pretty much nothing. Conrad Jupiters was how I was able to keep both shop doors open and maintain paying my bills to the best of my ability, considering the circumstances.

    Trying to detect the source of daily losses from each shop proved fruitless and as close to impossible as you could get. One thing for sure though, as the stress continuously grew greater, my hair became increasingly grey. Our Gold Coast Highway outlet was owned by an Australian couple,

---

6. Panadeine Forte contains paracetamol and codeine and is commonly used to relieve moderate to severe pain and fever.

Ross and Elva Henderson. The most down to earth people you could ever meet in a single lifetime and so easy to deal with, quite the opposite to Yung. Over a five-year period we fell behind in the rent several times and they would work with us to fix and solve the financial cash flow woes one endures in running a small business. Together we would always resolve the problem in an adult, business-like and civil manner. Eventually we sold to a couple wanting to try their hand in small business for the first time. They went on to be very successful and ended up opening a second outlet. Eventually our small business adventure came to an end in May/June 2006.

Thank god for that. A time in our lives that we were happy to move forward from, but with absolutely no regrets and extremely grateful for the opportunity as well as the massive learning curve we experienced in operating retail outlets for just on 10 years; savage but pleasantly happy with our achievements in the simple fact that we were able to sell both businesses and not walk away from them as we all know so many are sadly forced to do.

Jeremy Smith

8

POPPY SEEDS AND WATERMELONS

27 November 2016

Moving on from the small business world I started contracting myself out as a contract 'pastry chef/cook'. I happily did this from early 2006 until late 2008 making a great many friends along the way, some of the greatest human beings I would ever meet. Most of them anyway. Real down-to-earth, sincere human beings. Except for one person who we'll call William, one of the biggest cockheads I have ever met or had anything to do with. An ego bigger than the Q1 located in Surfers Paradise. A chef that struggled to boil water and scramble eggs. Believe it or not he managed the kitchen in a local Queensland reputable golf course resort which was where I met him. He would get his just desserts in the end, pardon the pun. He had terminated me after 2 ½ years for no apparent reason and later from an external position, I too would have him terminated. The day that it happened all my work colleagues who I engaged with kept my mobile phone running 'red hot'. For about a week I laughed so hard I thought I was going to have to see my abdominal surgeon, I really started to think I had torn some of the many hernias that I have had repaired over the years. Yes, it was just chronic soreness of the stomach muscles. I had never laughed so hard. The golf resort boys said on the initial first loudspeaker phone call, "He's been fired and he's roaming around the kitchen screaming your name and continuously 'fuck' and 'cunt'". I thought it was priceless. One of the most achievable things with which I have ever been involved. This arsehole had fired 40–50 full-time staff in a staggering 12-month period. It was disgraceful, even the general manager was scared of him because of his aggression and his onsite violence in the workplace. Someone had to stop him, and I was extremely happy to be that 'someone'. He was very well known to Queensland police as well I might add. But yes, you guessed it, the good old 'Ice'[7] was responsible. One of the boys, Holmesly, said on the phone to me, "Mate, you have balls bigger than watermelons". And I replied, "Yes, and most have balls the size of poppyseeds and he is one of them." I guess

---

7. Ice is Australian slang for methamphetamines, also known as 'crystal meth'.

that's what happens when you play with food for 30 years. Some of us, not many – about 5% – swallow watermelon seeds and the other 95% swallow poppyseeds. And yes, this sorts the boys from the men.

Until you have worked in a high pressure commercial kitchen environment, you can only really try and imagine how aggressive and abusive these places can be. Way worse than your average not so great building site. But it does make you see things in a completely different light than that of the 'Average Joe', 38-hours-per-week worker who never really gets their hands dirty. It certainly makes you a tougher, much stronger individual who doesn't back down from what is right from wrong.

29 November 2016

Over the years, since the young age of six, I have had some of the most bizarre personal injuries, some of which are based on my 100-mph personality, nature and zest for life. Some of these are as follows:

1. At six years old my mother bought me a new pair of corduroy trousers which I couldn't get on quick enough and yes, you guessed it, no undies. And yep, got the crown jewels caught in the zipper. Off to the

Byron Bay hospital with the now destroyed trousers with only the crutch part and zipper hanging from the neck and giblets.

2. At age 11–12 in the basement of Mullumbimby High School, northern NSW, while playing handball with my mates, a 1 ½ inch long screw hanging out of the high school canteen bench drove into my head. The doctor, Jim Hounslow, had this to say, "What were you doing having a screw under the bench anyway in only year 7 at high school?"

3. Hanging momentarily from the steel mesh basketball net, I got stuck on one of the steel knots in the net, and then fell quickly to the ground. Yep, still have the scar to prove it on the 'special finger' known as the 'rude finger' by some, namely my two sons, Jack and Harry. Painful? YES! Did it stop me? NO! Doctor/school nurse Mrs Nola McMahon at Mullumbimby High had these words, "I don't like the sight of blood".

4. A ¾-inch camphor laurel wood splinter went straight from the bench circular saw through my eyeball in woodwork at Mullum High. Doctor unknown but removed cornea in Mullumbimby hospital to successfully remove the piece of wood. That bastard of an eyeball burned for a week, thanks to the bloody

camphor laurel oil from the timber. Permanent damage? Extremely lucky, none.
5. This is a personal favourite but was unbelievably embarrassing at the time. Can you believe at about age 13 years a paralysis tick embedded in my ball bag? Yep, camping with 'Big Gav' at Clarkes Beach Caravan Park, Byron Bay. The doctor was Joan Nichols, Big Gav's mum. Yep, there I was sitting there in the tent with my scrotum in her hand with a bloody big pair of tweezers trying to get this burrowing little bastard out, and finally a good dab of metho to make sure she killed any remains. That brought a whole new meaning to the word burning.
6. Sliced thumb open on the 'Pal' can feeding one of my best mates Rocky, my purebred collie.
7. While trying to retrieve my Suzuki GSX-R 750 just to go for a quick blast, sliced four fingers on the left hand on the garden shed panels inside the single garage on Kingsley Street, Byron Bay.
8. Cut hand in half at Byron Bay Hot Bread Kitchen. Two fingers went one way and two fingers the other way. Nine needles later and several stitches.
9. Age 21, displaced fibular that three general practitioners could not diagnose. Finally, some 2 ½ weeks

later, good old Jimmy Hounslow diagnosed a badly displaced fibular leg bone.
10. Several hernia operations (five in total).
11. Severely torn ligaments in the left foot and ankle at 14 years of age. Completely unable to bear weight for approximately four weeks; not allowed medical help due to Rex Smith's deranged thought pattern.
12. Sliced the side of the wrist through to the bone, on a self-cutting pie tin at O'Reilly's Mountain Retreat.

Jeremy Smith

9

A WILD AND ROUGH RIDE

22 December 2016
Accident Number 13. 25 October 2008, approx. 3.45 p.m.

It has taken me approximately four years to actually put pen to paper about this next accident. And there were many more to list other than this, but I just selected the most bizarre ones, this final one being the most severe and life changing. This accident is clearly stamped in my mind forever and yes, I can and will continue to remember it like yesterday for the rest of my life. I am seriously struggling to make my hand push this pen and my emotions are running wild as I write. But I do know deep down in my heart that this is the best therapy not only for me but anyone who has had a life-changing event resulting in major trauma and permanent physical disability. As those goosebumps start to stand out on every square inch of my body, I can see that Saturday arvo on 25 October at the approximate time of 3.45 p.m. was where I would begin the wildest and roughest ride of my life.

I had taken my wife and three children and parents up to O'Reilly's Rain Forest Retreat in the Lamington National Parks QLD to experience a beautiful weekend at one of the brand new, state-of-the-art villas; there were 48 of them to be exact, which had been established and developed by the O'Reilly families with whom I had a very good relationship as I had done kitchen contract work for them in their many mountaintop food and beverage outlets. Vanessa, our two eldest children and I participated in the adventure ride of the O'Reilly's 'Flying Fox'. The two eldest children, then aged seven and nine, loved their first ride on the Flying Fox, approximately 120–130 metres long. My parents watched on with our 19-month-old son – the youngest of the three – on the luscious grass below. At the end of the first ride after overcoming their many fears, the two children Georgia and Harry were so excited they begged and pleaded me to take them back up for a second go, as did pretty much every kid. Reluctantly, only because of the tiring mountain climb back up to the Flying Fox, I quickly gave in – as you do – and said, "Come on kids, off we go, let's go and have some fun". We waited in line for our turn as it was fairly steady with willing participants, and as I would go first this time the same as the initial turn, I said to the operator Duncan who understood my need for speed, "How do I go faster?" He replied, "Just run and jump out off the launch ramp in a long jump style approach". So I did. This, at the age of 37, would be the last day I would ever walk on two legs unaided. I crashed into the side of the mountain, propelled up and then downwards with the most horrendous and excessive force from the steel cable on which we were riding which has a double pulley harness style system rigged to a safety jacket. I immediately snapped the side of my right calcaneus/heel bone, and not known then at first but had in fact completely crushed my entire central foot and ankle joints; this would be the beginning for me of a seriously rough ride, yes literally.

The decision that I took running down that launch ramp and jumping off to get more speed was something that I have struggled to deal with. As the extent of the injury was unbeknown, other than massive amounts of agonising and excruciating levels of pain, we stayed on to enjoy Saturday night. The family hounded me to leave the mountain as soon as possible and seek immediate medical help at one of the local Gold Coast hospitals, as my whole right leg began to swell excessively, without showing any signs of slowing. So, me being me, said selflessly, "No, we will stay, I am not buggering up everyone's weekend over an injured ankle". I had spoken. The whole right foot and ankle was in such excruciating pain, one just can't explain, this is something you would need to experience yourself to try and understand 100 percent. Most of the pain had happened in my childhood years up to about 15–16 years of age.

In life to date at age 37 I had already experienced some very different forms of pain, from being 'screwed' under the canteen counter bench at Mullumbimby High School to being speared in the eyeball with a camphor laurel splinter, and then an aggressive little paralysis tick chewing on my scrotum laced with metho along with some other little rippers, but I must say – please pardon the pun – this did take the cake, icing and all.

First thing on the Sunday morning 26 October 2008 we quickly packed up and left as the leg had gotten worse overnight, both pain and swelling wise. Then we remembered that I had my motorbike up at the back of the main kitchen, and yep you guessed it, nobody had a licence to ride it home for me, and as I predicted I would be off work for a couple of weeks and was never going to leave one of my most prized possessions outside on the mountain for any length of time, I agonisingly threw my leg over and rode the bike home to the coast one hour and 15 minutes away. That time off work ended up just on three months.

Jeremy Smith

26 December 2016

This time of year, from 15 December and every Christmas from this date moving forward would now always be an awkward struggle for me, thanks to the incident and the infamous Rex Smith and yes, the super bitch, my sister, Karen Justice, too. Something I would, for the rest of my life, never really understand, I just wanted to make the best of what I had to work with, having always been a super emotional and seriously passionate human being, and that serious zest for life I had always had since the age of seven. An irreversible date of a true living disastrous nightmare... just when you thought things couldn't get any worse, they could and, in fact, did. 15 December 2013. I will come back to it, let's get back to the comical playout at the Robina Hospital, Queensland.

9 January 2017

We arrived at the Robina Hospital, QLD, after putting the Suzuki to rest under its covers at about 10.00 a.m. on 26 October 2008 and, as I approached the bench – triage desk that is – the nurse said, "What have you done?" And I replied, "You are going to think I am a dickhead, but I have only just found out that we have a heel bone and I think I might have broken mine". "Impossible." she said. "Oh, sorry love," I replied, "can't break the heel bone?" "Yes, you can," she said, "but it is impossible to walk in here the way you did". "What, like a ballerina?" I replied. She continued to tell me that the pain threshold was way too intense for the brain to manage/handle. I said, "Fair enough, probably just soft tissue damage, resulting in a pretty bad sprain, but anyway you people are the experts, I am just a cook." She quickly asked me the stock standard question: "Pain out of 10?" I replied agonisingly with a dead straight face, "11–12". She looked at my wife Vanessa and said, "Is he joking or is he serious?" Vanessa replied, "No, he is deadly serious, it's probably a 13, but he will never let on, he will never show it in his face, that's just the way he is... and joking or serious, that's the way he has always been, he likes to keep people guessing, that is just him". Here come those bloody goosebumps again, I'm covered from head to toe over this part of my story and the song on the radio as I write is *Dancin' On My Own* by Calum Scott. Quickly three of the female nurses threw me into a wheelchair and whipped me off to the X-ray room for foot photos. I had always hated photos, but this was only of the foot and ankle, no ugly dial[8] involved as Wally Hooker always told me.

---

8. Australian slang for 'face'.

Before I knew it, the entire room was full of hotshots and once I started seeing those fancy suits I knew this was no ankle sprain. The nurses said that we were just waiting on the two orthopods to come and see me, 'Orthopods,' I thought, 'What in the fuck is going on?' Clearly, I had never heard this terminology before as I had always tried my hardest to avoid doctors and especially hospitals. I quickly worked out this was their slang for an orthopaedic specialist surgeon. The girls soon went on to tell me it was likely I would need surgery, I replied, "No need, just a bandage will suffice. I have got to get back to work ASAP, I have a mortgage to pay and a family to feed. What are we talking [about]," I asked the orthopods, "one week or two?" They looked at me completely blankly, with a look of despair that I couldn't quite explain. Then one of the senior ones said to me quietly, "Mate, you need a minimum of three months off your feet with 100% rest". 'Rest' was a word that I had never, ever really understood the actual meaning of; I knew at that instant we would lose our family home. The medical clan stood around chatting about my situation and discussing the surgery options with each other, looking at the many X-rays on the wall lamp. I overheard one of the now approximate 11 staff members say, "This bloke is mad, he wants to go back to work in a week or two with just a bandage on". "Hey! I heard that!" I responded and the whole room erupted in a burst of laughter, even the hotshots in those fancy suits were laughing. The young fellow and I soon engaged in conversation, and I said to him jokingly, "My fists still work and so does my size ten left boot". He laughed and quickly replied, "Sorry mate you are buggered you can't get me, you've got a fractured calcaneus, you are stuck there on that bed". The instantaneous look on those three nurses' faces was absolutely priceless, they looked at one another with amazement and then at breakneck speed one turned to him and said, "Oh he will get you alright, he has got a pain threshold like we have never seen before, he walked into the A & E with that smashed heel bone and the bastard will probably chase you down the corridor until he catches you, be careful mate". Quickly that X-ray room turned into a live stand-up comedy fest, crossed over with a cartoon similar to the *Road Runner* and *Wile E. Coyote*. It was seriously funny, super entertaining humour to us all, even me sitting there in agony; I think my pain lightened somewhat for the half an hour that the stage show lasted. The people in this room were a great bunch of human beings who somehow took the seriousness of my injury out of the medical equation – after all I had lived my life around numbers, this is how I remembered everything and anything.

The surgeons eventually decided that surgery wouldn't

be required. If only they knew what was about to unfold, what was lurking around that corner 12–14 months from this day moving forward. Finally, they plastered me in a knee-high cast and advised 3–4 months non-weight bearing on the foot to ensure a full recovery. 'That's it,' I said to myself, 'Our Mermaid Beach family home is history' always relying on my better than average foresight. It was a no-brainer really but somehow in my mind I knew I was going to be in for the fight of my life. My mind, my heart and soul just knew that this was more than just a crushed calcaneus/heel bone. You got it, my mind, heart and soul – which to date had never failed me – were spot on and my gut instinct was bulletproof. What was about to unfold would become my worst ever real living daily nightmare: 24/7 pain that I just couldn't get my head around, and my brain seriously struggled to deal with. My brain would cop the biggest pounding of its life, riddled with in and out of control excruciating and chronic pain 24 hours per day, seven days per week. Sleep became impossible due to the pain and discomfort and the constant worry on my mind daily with a wife and three children to support, was truly indescribable. How in the hell were we going to make ends meet, pay the mortgage, the bills and put food on the table seven days a week?

11 January 2017

After several consults with the Robina Hospital's so-called specialist orthopaedics team in the Outpatients Department, and after several dozens of heated discussions with the *Doogie Howser*[9] doctors over a period of some 13 months the diagnosis was a serious psychological injury rather than a serious physical injury. A minimum of no less than 20 different interns, at an average age of not more than 23–26, trained by senior doctors no more than 31–35 years of age, all proceeded to tell me that there was nothing wrong with either my left or right foot or ankles and that the fractured calcaneus was completely healed and I was back to 100% health.

As the pain in my right foot and ankle region began to seriously intensify over the next 10–13 months, eventually a female doctor told me to my face that I was telling myself in my mind that both my left and right foot and ankles were sore and quite painful but that, in fact, there was "nothing wrong with either of them, especially the left one," and she chuckled. And as she chuckled, I exploded and said, "Get me out of this shithole and send me up to the Southport Hospital

---

9. *Doogie Howser* was a very well-known American TV series about a young doctor who looked about 16–17 years of age.

where the real doctors are because I am more of a doctor than any of you clowns will ever be!" This happened with immediate effect.

Very quickly at the then Southport Hospital I was attended to by five public very senior orthopaedic surgeons. In charge of the team dealing with my condition was a man called Dr Don Pitchford, a lovely bloke with real concern and equal urgency for the horrendous amount of pain I was in, mostly with the right foot and ankle on the lateral side and in the central side of the lateral side of the foot. After approximately two weeks of unlimited numbers of X-rays and ultrasounds and various other tests and procedures, I was told by the senior surgeons that between the five of them they had never experienced such a traumatic foot ankle injury due to the rarity of this particular crushing style of trauma injury and that my injury was beyond their collective expertise; quite simply they said to me that it was out of their league. I truly did appreciate and respect their honesty. Don Pitchford came to me and said, "Jeremy, we are hiring a man from the private sector to help with your injury and his name is Aneel Nihal. This man is purely a foot and ankle specialist with 37 years' experience and is world renowned". Finally, I would be in the hands of, thank god, a man that was not only serious about what he did for a job but a man who was incredibly professional, passionate, caring and most of all an absolute perfectionist, in every form of the word. This bloke is a genuine, no bullshit, dinkum fair human being. Thankfully, things were finally starting to fall into place, the public system had given me a private specialist who knew what he was doing. My mind started to slightly ease somewhat, I was seriously struggling to believe it, the pain was simply indescribable; merely resting the foot on the floor with feather weight pressure caused me to smash two top teeth with two bottom teeth in a crocodile/Great White shark-like bite, weight bearing and trying to walk was just simply a whole different story

On the first consult with Dr Nihal he could visually see the swelling in the foot and ankle but didn't think it was abnormal, but what he could identify quite easily was the pain and distress in my face as I tried to weight bear and walk a step or two. He looked at – in his words as he stated into his dictaphone – the 3.5 kgs of imagery scans that I had undergone in the past 5–7 months which were substantial. He went on to report on his dictaphone that he had never before seen so many X-rays/scans and other tests, etc. in his entire career, and he found it incredibly hard to believe that the so-called specialists in the public system had repeatedly told me there was nothing wrong and that I simply had a major psychological rather than a major physical injury. After a very thorough investigation of those 3.5 kgs of X-rays he slowly but surely started to discover the tiniest but crucially important problems[10] on those many images taken by the consultants in the public sector.

On the second consult with him some ten days after our in-depth conversation during the initial visit, he looked at me and asked me to give him the best two words to describe the pain. I quickly responded and staring him straight in the face said, "Doctor, I don't know the best two words in the English language to describe the pain but I can tell you this; AGONISING and EXCRUCIATING do not exist in my vocabulary." And in that beaut ridgey-didge Indian accent he said, "Oh my god, this is going to be unbelievably challenging and testing". As he looked very closely at several of the radiographs on the wall lamp, he suddenly looked closer and then looking at me said quickly in that Indian accent, "I know what it is." "What is it?" I asked. He answered in the most serious tone; "I am 99.9% sure it is firstly a marrow oedema, and secondly, and very seriously," he said, "you have an avascular necrosis of the cuboid bone." I replied back, "What in the hell is that, please explain in layman's terms, I have no idea what you are talking about."

---

10. As Dr Nihal, who is a medical genius, looked closer he started to notice that there was bone shadowing that shouldn't have been there under normal conditions; though they were significant on the scans they were incredibly hard to spot as they were mere millimetres.

I was totally unaware of the seriousness of this medical condition; in layman's terms that fancy diagnosis meant that my cuboid bone was dying, or it was highly possible that it was already dead and riddled with infection. Dr Nihal then said I needed to undergo a quick physical examination just to confirm the diagnosis, he then screwed his right index finger with force into my cuboid bone, and though he did warn that it would be quite painful I just wasn't prepared for the intensity of what was about to come. He screwed that finger that hard into that rotten cuboid bone, I just screamed and screamed, cried uncontrollably and very unsurprisingly was swearing at the top of my lungs. My back, according to a family member was the shape of the Sydney Harbour Bridge, and as I crashed back into the wall, I am sure the entire orthopaedic ward was 100% convinced that someone was being murdered; well I can tell you this much I thought I was, and yes by a specialist doctor. My pain and crying were surprisingly uncontrollable as pain had never really bothered me all my life to date, but fuck me, this bothered me. As I regained my composure and got myself together and stopped sooking[11] Dr Nihal turned to me and said, "I will have to do it one more time for confirmation before I send you off

---

11. 'Sooking' refers to someone who is crying or moping over nothing really worthwhile, like a small toddler that has their food or toy taken from them.

to the Royal Brisbane and Women's Hospital for a bone scan and a bone density scan first thing in the morning." I said, "Doctor if you do that again I will probably knock you out." He quickly looked at the family member with me who said, "Dr Nihal if he said he will knock you out, then more than likely he will." I said to Dr Nihal, "I will only get you with a quick soft left jab but not intentionally, it will just be a knee-jerk reaction due to that excruciating pain you are inflicting upon me, but yes, a soft one will still put you to sleep, something that is completely foreign to me." "Oh my god," Dr Nihal replied in that priceless Indian accent, "I don't want to be getting knocked out." "Okay," he said, "I will be very gentle this time." "Please, please, please." I replied still trying to get my breath back from the first lot of physical torture. The family member went on to say, "Dr Nihal he has been in this pain of disbelief for in excess of 9–10 months now." And I said, "That's thanks to those orthopaedic specialist clowns at the Robina Hospital".

    He proceeded to press the site again with the utmost featherlike touch, only slightly pressing on the skin and bone, and the exact same thing happened instantly, all over again. "Yes, my diagnosis is correct," he said, "that cuboid bone needs urgent immediate surgery once we confirm with the various bone scan radiograph results."

17 January 2017

I looked at him and said directly to his face, "Forget the scans, just get that thing out of my foot, no need for the anaesthetist, just grab a knife from the lunch room and get the bastard out, it is destroying me." And yes, it was, literally. I said to him, "No need to wash it, a little vegemite has never killed anybody, just get the prick of a thing out so I can get out of this soul-destroying pain, it's killing me." The very next day I found myself travelling to the Royal Brisbane and Women's Hospital where I underwent extensive scans for approximately two hours purely for medical evidence and confirmation of Dr Nihal's diagnosis. Even with chronic life-threatening depression beyond belief – purely from severe chronic pain and eventual financial ruin – I knew I would inevitably end up relying on my better than average foresight and really began to understand the extent of my injury. I just would never have imagined in my wildest dreams that I would be in for the biggest 8–9-year battle of my life; yes, a serious and unimaginable fight against severe, chronic and debilitating pain, both physically and mentally. This for me, I thought, would be the biggest challenge of my life, however, it turned out that I was totally wrong. I had an even higher hurdle that I was going to have to face, at this stage totally unbeknown to me; a hurdle that I was seriously going to struggle to get over, but I just had to keep punching on.

After the two hours of scans I was surrounded by no less than 10–12 radiology staff, begging and pleading with them to give me the results, especially of my bone density scan, but they whispered in confidence constantly about my pictures. I fell in and out of sleep on the scanning bed from sheer exhaustion from that hard-to-believe excruciating pain from this mongrel right foot and ankle. As I drifted in and out of sleep, I repeatedly asked them for my results and they just kept replying with those blank faces, "You will have to talk to your specialist." My frustration and anger kept forcing me back to sleep; I just wanted to know and I just wanted this pain gone ASAP. I didn't want to own it for a second more than I had to.

10

THE FIGHT OF MY LIFE

Two days later at 6.30 a.m. I found myself in an operating theatre in the Gold Coast Southport Hospital, under the care of Dr Aneel Nihal and his public team of theatre staff to fix and repair the problem with this bone. At this stage I still hadn't been told of the seriousness of this particular bone condition, I had no idea I was up against a life or death situation, but one thing I was sure of, I knew how to keep fighting. The procedure carried out by Dr Nihal was that of a bone graft from my right tibia into the cuboid bone shell which was still in good shape and order. The complete bone marrow removal of the cuboid was unavoidable as the bone was completely rotten, dead and red hot with infection.

On 18 January 2011, the very next day Dr Nihal visited me bedside first thing that morning at 7.30 a.m. and proceeded to tell me that I was the luckiest man on the planet today. Not understanding the seriousness of the life or death situation I asked him "Why, Dr Nihal why?" He proceeded to tell me in intricate detail that the night before while sitting with his wife at the dinner table he began to tell her he had a 39-year-old male with a wife and three children on whom he was to perform surgery first thing in the morning on 17 January who had the worst bone density scan results he had seen in 37 years of medical practice. He then told me that he had discussed with his wife the seriousness of my chronic depression due to severe and chronic levels of pain 24/7 and going through financial ruin as we speak, caused by the injury and lack of income capacity as I was unable to walk or bear weight let alone work. "Please love, tell me before I put him to sleep at 7.00 a.m. in the morning, do I or do I not tell him that it's likely, 95% plus that I will have to cut his leg off below the knee to save his life, based on the worst bone scan results I have ever seen in 37 years, and if I do," he said to his wife, "the shock will most definitely kill him based on his very low and poor state of mind." She reacted at lightning bolt speed and said, "Aneel, let us pray," and she bowed her head as did he and they both closed their eyes together and she said to her husband, "Let us pray to god for nothing other than a medical miracle." "And we got one," he said to me quite teary-eyed. It was at that moment that each and every single goose bump and hair stood end to end on my entire body and today, 3 February 2017, as I write they still do; my emotions run wild, supercharged throughout my body, I must say right now at this minute my tears are nothing but those of solemn joy, but fuck me it has been an out of control unbelievably hard road.

I sincerely thank you Dr Nihal and especially you Mrs Nihal, for your miraculous and magical prayer from the deepest depths of my heart. Dr Nihal, you are a man who will hold a special place in my heart and mind for the rest of my life. I will never forget them – him or her – because quite simply they both kept me above ground and for that I will always be forever grateful. Before Dr Nihal left my bedside to attend to other patients, he said, "May I ask you one personal question?" and I said, "Dr Nihal absolutely ask me whatever you want." He said, "Would you be known to have somewhat unbelievable amounts of mongrel determination?" I just laughed a little and said, "You will have to ask my mates that one." He smiled and in that priceless Indian accent said, "I will take that as a yes," and he said directly to my face, "I just want you to know that that is quite simply what kept you alive." He shook my hand and left, giving me something even more to absorb and comprehend in full, all I knew was that I was a fighter indeed.

I just need a quick break for a coffee and my arrowroot bickies, I knew this would be the hardest part of my story, but it has hit my emotional department like a ton of bricks,

I will be back shortly, I just need to get myself back together. Thank you for your patience.

3 February 2017

Okay I'm all good. I feel so much better now and getting stronger by the day, slowly but surely. Two years ago, I was a very weak 253[12], but over this last 15–17 months I am on my way back to a beautifully tuned 308[13] with minor splits in the plug leads. So, let's continue. After approximately 7–10 days I was in the clear having avoided septicaemia and gangrene thanks to the legendary medical god and genius Dr Aneel Nihal, but severe and chronic pain were still seriously persistent but absolutely not the slightest bit comparable to that of the pain from that mongrel cuboid bone.

Dr Nihal resigned with immediate effect some days later from the public sector over my treatment. He showed me some of the medical notes; it was seriously hard to believe, he explained that this was why he worked only in the private sector. I said to him, "Doctor I completely understand, I am just glad you managed to keep me out of a long pine box and to me that's all that matters." We shook hands firmly for the

---

12. Smallest V8 engine Australia has ever produced.
13. A larger V8 than that of the 253.

final time in the plaster room and he left with flames firing out of both ears and heavily from both nostrils; this man made me feel really good as I was as passionate as he, and had his same perfectionist type and style of personality, but I only mixed flour and water for a living, whereas he played with people's lives daily. I could completely 100% really relate to his level of anger as he stormed out of the room.

Jeremy Smith

11

THE SCOTTISH GENTLEMAN

My new surgeon Dr Matthew Hope was a Scotsman born in Glasgow, the same place as my mum. He now took over the orthopaedic mess of my right foot and ankle. He would eventually discover – after some very serious study of the many radiographs that he had requested after my initial surgery, due to the many changes that can occur after disturbance by any surgery – that the now newly rebuilt cuboid bone was grinding away together with the calcaneus (heel) bone, rubbing themselves away on each other due to the space closure caused by the horrendous force from the initial Flying Fox accident. At this point I didn't realise the complexity of this crushing injury or that I would be about to participate in the roughest and wildest ride of my life, trying eagerly to distract my mind through the study of law and money markets and my continuous browsing of cars and motorbikes online and yes, worst of all, the very messy and controversial Australian politics, watching the Rudd and Gillard government completely destroy this wonderful country of ours, Australia. And the fall of many corporate giants showing significant forms of failure in the business sectors locally and globally. This was only the beginning of the aftermath of the global financial disaster (GFC) in more ways than one and also the beginning for me of a rough ride that I would have preferred to have sat on the sideline and simply watched.

Feeling massive bouts of disbelief through chronic, severe and disabling pain of this mongrel foot, facing financial ruin including bankruptcy and the financial parasites breathing down my neck daily, eventually I hit the lowest ever point in my life. The loss of our family home in Mermaid Beach on the Gold Coast, Queensland was a real game breaker. I had hit absolute rock bottom. On 18 October 2011 day my wife and I declared ourselves bankrupt and surrendered our house back to the Westpac Banking Corporation. This broke the whole family's heart and started breaking the actual family itself. Me and my out-of-control extreme levels of pain made for a very awkward way of life for my wife and three children. I became close to impossible to live with, and with very little help from either of our families, this was an almost impossible journey for anyone, not just us.

I had already slipped into a fairly chronic form of clinical depression, struggling majorly on a daily basis with incredibly strong thoughts and ideas of suicide every minute of every day. This was purely to escape these outrageous levels of chronic and debilitating pain, not to mention the guilt I was drowning in for being the main cause of the loss of our Mermaid Beach family home. My big picture and long-term plan had been detonated and a big part of me had been detonated as well. As time went by, I would undergo a further four fairly major and intricate type surgeries thanks to the fabulous and amazingly humble Dr Matthew Hope, to date he is in my Top 5 best ever human beings I have ever met. I felt very calm being in his surgical care for nearly seven years as he was always professional and always tried to make light of my crippling situation and hence his name; he gave me hope in the now tricky position I found myself in. The surgeries he performed on my right foot and ankle included:

- Fusion of the right calcaneus bone to the cuboid bone.
- Triple arthrodesis of foot and ankle.
- Removal of Bassett ligament and an arthroscopic debridement.
- Peroneal tendon tenolysis and division of the sural nerve and removal from foot, with a relocation to the calf muscle region.

After 6 ½ years of surgery after surgery I found myself 97% mentally spent and started to realise a substantial change within myself – mentally, physically and most of all, emotionally. Everything that had happened thus far had finally taken its toll on me, I honestly felt like I had been run over by not one but two B-Doubles[14]. The only real positive to come from all of this was quite likely that I was still alive, but only just, those suicidal thoughts would sneak back in slowly but surely and they would continue to linger thanks, many thanks to my infamous deranged sister and my absolute cockhead father.

I eventually finally suffered a major nervous breakdown in January 2014. This was the final straw. I'd been broken 100% thanks to my own wife and family and I must mention none other than QLD mental health, and mostly thanks to the infamous psychiatric consultant Doctor Haritha Devineni. Let me tell you she was anything but divine as her surname somewhat suggests.

---

14. Oversized semi-trailer truck (Aus).

Jeremy Smith

12

KICKED WHILE YOU'RE DOWN

16 March 2017

As mentioned earlier in the story, just when I thought it wasn't possible for things to sink any lower. In fact, I truly didn't believe it was possible for things to get any tougher for me at the age now of only 42 years young, but on the 15th December 2013 my ultimate disbelief came to real-life fruition when my own flesh and blood had a mental health court order served on me. Yep, fully instigated by my now – and then – infamous deranged sister and yep, the most piss weak man I had ever met in my life, the incredibly dishonest, weak, pathetic and most of all cowardly father, Rex Stanley Smith. The two masterminds behind the court order, who constantly got in the way of me living my life for myself rather than either of them; that fucking pair of manipulative, dishonest, lying, fabricating and most of all, two of the biggest ever drama, attention-seeking arseholes I had ever met in my life. Two people who could convince anyone of anything purely through their sickening change in tone of voice. These two particular human beings thrived on embellishment and could quickly turn a molehill into a mountain and yep, you guessed it, both ex-NSW government workers who thought their shit had absolutely no odour.

So, if I can remember rightly on the evening of either the 12th or 13th December 2013 I found myself being ambushed as I arrived home from work at approximately 7.00 p.m. at night. I found it quite odd that my nephew Ben was at my home in Mermaid Waters and my then wife had been constantly ringing me as I was on my way home from my job in the Gold Coast hinterland. The many attempts to ring me were extremely excessive and when I arrived home I suddenly began to smell the strongest scent of a very large rat. I walked in the back door with my workmate Steve who had given me a lift to the Gold Coast and I had offered him a drink in return so that he could quickly meet with Vanessa and my three children. I just knew as we all sat to enjoy a drink together that something just wasn't quite right as both Vanessa and Ben both seemed incredibly on edge. It wasn't more than 35 minutes before the Queensland mental health officers turned up at the back door we had just walked through. As I approached the back door to see who Vanessa was talking to it was at that moment, I spotted the two QLD government badges. There were two QLD government officials from the Southport Magistrates Court, one male and one female, but at least they were well-mannered. I ran a quick assessment and said to them, "Who are you?" They replied, "Are you Jeremy Rex Smith 25-7-71?" "Yes, I am," I replied, "I don't exactly know you are, but I can tell you, fuck I am angry." And truly I was. They proceeded to tell me their position with the Southport Magistrates Court and that they were from the mental health sector. They asked if they could come in, and I replied, "Yes you can, but what have I done?" They quickly replied, "You have been driving erratically." And my blood instantly hit boiling point and my anger levels just about blew the roof tiles off the house. "What a load of fucking bullshit," I replied. "I took my new car for a drive with my sister's then soft cock boyfriend [one of the many on the list of suckers] with my 12-year-old son, Harry."

I had simply put my foot down on the gas for no more than seven seconds in an unrestricted speed zone, one of only two or three left in Australia, the others of which are somewhere in the Northern Territory. This was together with a mate of mine heavily associated with GMH Australia to talk – and talk only – about my current situation financially and a lifetime dream of wanting to race cars. And now this had turned into a real living nightmare that I just didn't need thanks to two fuckwits that I had never really thought much of to be quite honest, my own father and sister. I knew of other family members and a seriously long list of human beings that also weren't real big fans of these two particular dickheads: two people who thought they were really something special in society purely, I believe, because of their past NSW government background. But really and honestly, they were just two mainstream, below average, dead shit human beings who had no real purpose in this world; both were sensational human failures and simply nothing else. As had been said by previous family members, they were constantly playing the blame game with anyone and everyone closest to them quite simply to make them feel better about themselves and nothing else; this was a massive part of their false sense of power. Two people – the only two people that I knew in this world that were never wrong, classical signs of government employees. And who, through majorly chronic lies and deceit, could get themselves out of the deepest shit and were very capable of putting somebody else into the shit that just couldn't possibly get any deeper. These two people were human beings the world could do without, and I must say that my giggles and laughter to this day make me feel great about how piss weak their characters both were.

So, these mental health officials went on with quite an interrogation style of interview that lasted for around one hour and 20 minutes. I was like a raging bull when we near the end of the very interrogative and humiliating interview. They finished up by demanding that I see a QLD government psychiatrist the very next day and then told me that the order was a legal document and, according to the court, I had to do as I was told. I replied, "I don't give a shit what it is, I won't be seeing anyone and I won't be told what to do by anyone, especially when I haven't done anything wrong, and especially when I haven't broken any laws!"

Finally, they returned to their taxpayer funded car and left to go back to the rock that they had crawled out from under. What a job, and what a waste of hard-earned, working taxpayers' money. Public servants purely just wasting good money; if I could have explained half a lifetime of abuse and neglect to these people in the time given, I quite simply would have. But this was most certainly impossible, and it was then that I made a very firm and frank decision to write a book, something that people from all walks of life had been telling me to do for years, mainly work colleagues and a select few socially that had in some way become close to me, upfront and personal in a way, sharing our many stories with one another. I guess I just had to wait for the perfect timing and that perfect timing is now.

So, moving on with the QLD government and the court order, I had their demand that I was supposed to follow in my mind, but I just thought, 'Here go these cunts again, telling and giving misleading advice to not one, but two governments, the NSW people and the QLD government people.' So the following day I rang the QLD mental health number and told them that if I needed help, I would happily ask them for it, and to piss off and leave me alone. I explained that I had been to hell and back with a right foot and ankle injury which at this stage had taken approximately five years to rebuild thus far through several fairly extensive surgery procedures. I said to them again from Level Five inside the Jupiters Casino from where I made the phone call, "If you don't back off I will sue you, and I won't let up until I have." I didn't give a shit about the legal costs; I was and always have been a principled man and nothing other. I explained that I had done absolutely nothing wrong and that when they could produce evidence to suggest that I have, I would abide by all of their many stringent and strict rules and regulations and legislations, etc. but until then they should just piss off and leave me in peace, "because quite simply that is all I want, just my own time to try and heal and my way only, and nothing other than just that."

Jeremy Smith

5 April 2017

The thing that made me rage with anger was the simple fact of chronic lies and manipulation of words around the truth, the whole truth and nothing but the truth. What had been going on under our family's roof only we knew and especially only me. But together with many different pressures from my somewhat delusional family with their extremely dishonest comments and the many fabrications made about me to the QLD mental health people I found myself in a no-win situation. On the following day – 13 December 2013 – many of the Broadbeach Police were after me. My then neighbours approached me in a complete panic several times over a short period of time and asked me, "Have you killed somebody mate?" My very firm reply was, "No not yet, but it is a strong possibility, there is a fair chance it will happen."

Eventually I called the Broadbeach Police on the evening of 14 December 2013 and informed them who I was and told them that I would come willingly without any resistance or aggression. I asked them politely to please send only two coppers, otherwise I would find it extremely intimidating and confrontational, not to mention the embarrassment and humiliation I was already feeling within, knowing full well what the many neighbours would already be thinking after several attempts and searches to bring me in.

I was overwhelmed with a complete feeling of emptiness

and disbelief; I just couldn't fathom what was happening after being dumped in the shit by several family members and without being able to give my version of events as I had been stripped of every single liberty. The government and the court had chosen to believe a bunch of manipulating and controlling liars and as you know, us men have absolutely no rights whatsoever. With a zero-criminal history, an absolutely perfect clean record with the law apart from four or five basic speeding fines over 30 odd years, I was quickly made to feel like the terrorising and psychopathic lunatic, Ivan Milat[15]. It was overkill like I had never seen before, the way I was treated was somewhat like a Milat style serial killer. I just couldn't comprehend any of it when all I ever wanted was to fulfil a lifetime dream of wanting to race cars, something I had wanted to do since age four, a passion I can't quite explain, and those few that could relate, were my select group of lifelong mates, blokes that shared the same passion as me, but on a much lighter scale. The feeling was stronger than ever within me, I guess wholly and solely due to my near-death experience due to the misdiagnosis of the dead bone in my right foot and ankle, thanks to the outpatient circus clowns at the Robina Hospital, QLD.

With a major disability to the right leg, and the severe

---

15. Serial killer in NSW, Australia (1989–1993).

trauma from the many surgeries I had to undergo, my brain went into the biggest scramble it had ever been in, just a major massive tsunami of disbelief; the disability had forcefully and very powerfully made me understand what the most important things in my life were apart from my three beautiful children, and that was quite simply that I had a head over heels love and passionate desire to race cars, I seriously wanted to do this and tick it off my bucket list, after such a near and very serious flirt with death. My priorities in life had put themselves into serious order. My heart and my mind had given me the most in-depth and concerning auto reality check; in essence, I had put my priorities in order.

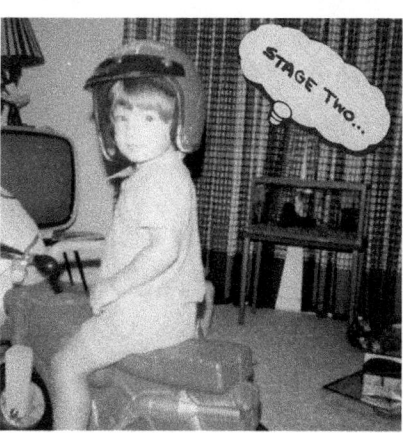

LOCAL NEWS

News feature

SECRET REVEALED: Rex Smith, pictured with his wife Marjorie and a black and white photo (also on opposite page) of the man he has been told is his biological father. Rex's mother Delma (pictured with a young Rex, below left) didn't tell him her husband Fred wasn't his father. Rex is now trying to find his biological father, Dallas Morgan, a serviceman who had been based at the RAAF training station at Evans Head.

PHOTO: GARY CHIGWIDDEN

...ed and Delma knew ...e other and he was appa-ly "keen" on her.
...hey were married in July, ... and shortly after, Fred sent to New Guinea ...re he served until the ...ended.
...ex was born on November 19, 1943 at a long-gone ...ore private hospital ... Delma swearing all ...ily members to secrecy ...t the circumstances of ...irth.
...nd given that Fred and ...na each came from 10-...ren families, it's re-...kable the secret was ...r revealed to Rex over ...e 68 years.
...hen Fred returned home ...945, he and Delma set up ...e in Little Keen Street, ...ore then later in Brun-...k Street and in 1947, ...na gave birth to a ...ghter, Rex's only sibling.
...ex recalls Fred was an ...redible" worker, at times ...ling down three jobs,

including one as a labourer with Lismore Council.
"He was a regular father. Went to work, came home. Drank and smoked a lot," said Rex.
"I turned out to be a bit of a sportsman from as young as I can remember and played every sport I could.
"Looking back I recall how he didn't want to go to many of my sporting events. I'm not putting him down. I just see it a lot clearer now.
"He never whacked me. It was my mother who was the real disciplinarian. Maybe she had told him he was not to touch me.
"It has taken this news for me to see now that he sort of stood in the background.
"That's the way he treated me until I went away."
While Rex, who left home at 15 to join the Bank of NSW (Westpac), said while they were never close he could not recall one incident that would have made him

suspect Fred wasn't his father.
His search for his biological father, including checks of RAAF service records in Canberra, births, deaths and marriages records, newspaper death notices and ancestry.com found no trace of a Dallas Morgan.
The task was made more difficult when Rex learned that apart from basic service records and some course photographs from that time, all records of courses and who had participated in them at the Evans Head training station, were dumped at sea after the war.
Dr Richard Gates, president of both the Evans Head Living Museum and the Evans Head Memorial Aerodrome Committee, who has been helping Rex in his search, said 5500 servicemen trained at what was known as the No.1 Bombing and Gunnery School and later the No.1 Air Observers

School at Evans Head during the war.
He said 1100 of those men were killed during the war and only about 100 of them were still alive.
After speaking to one of those surviving men now living on the Gold Coast, and given the lack of success over finding any mention of a Dallas Morgan in official records, Rex is not discounting the idea the name was false.
The former serviceman, whose name Rex didn't want to be made public to protect him from any possible embarrassment, said he was aware of some servicemen at the time giving false names when chatting up girls. The man, now in his 90s, said he had not heard of a Dallas Morgan while training at Evans Head.
Dr Gates, who is still following new leads for Rex, didn't believe giving a false name was a common practice among servicemen, but "it did happen".
Rex hasn't given up hope of discovering his father's real name and finding out whether he had a family of his own.
He really hopes someone will recognise the man in the photograph.
"I'm really hoping to find out if I have more brothers and sisters," he said.

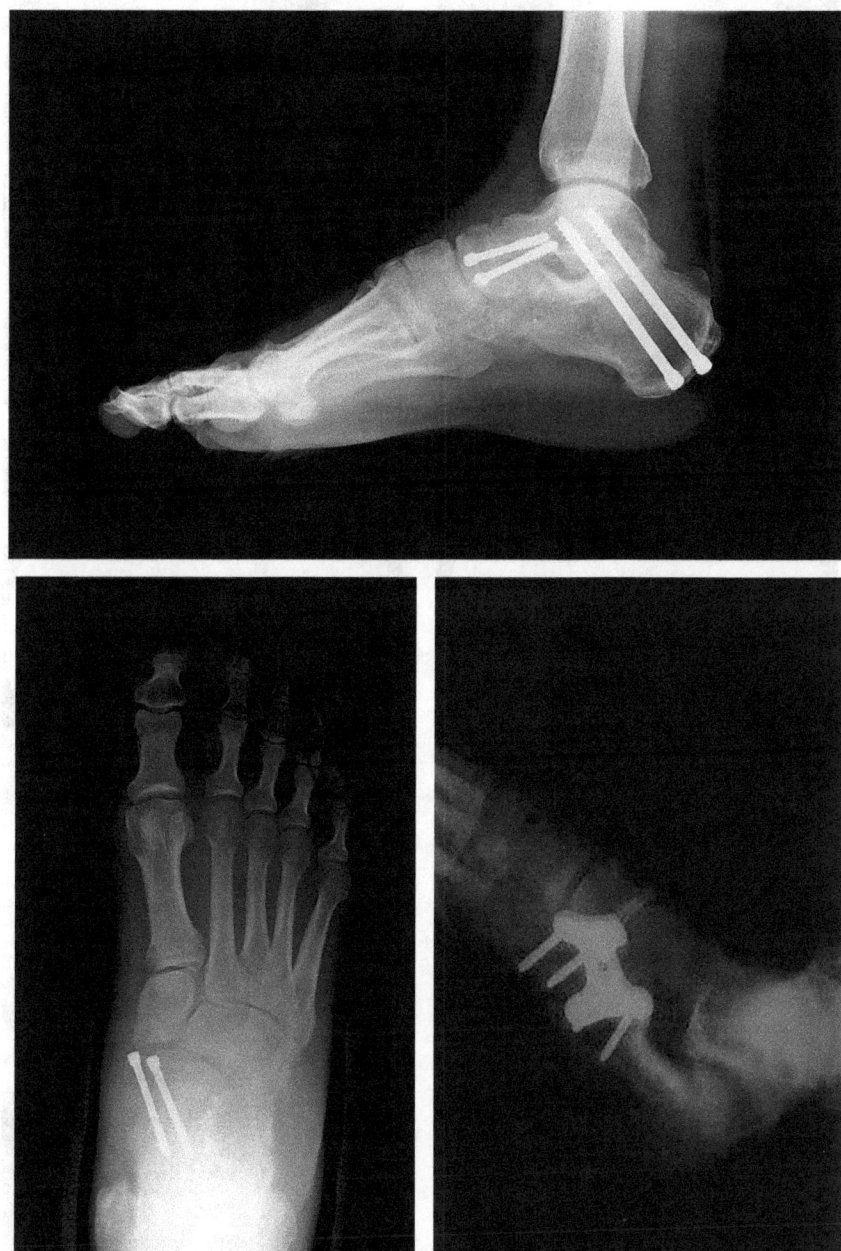

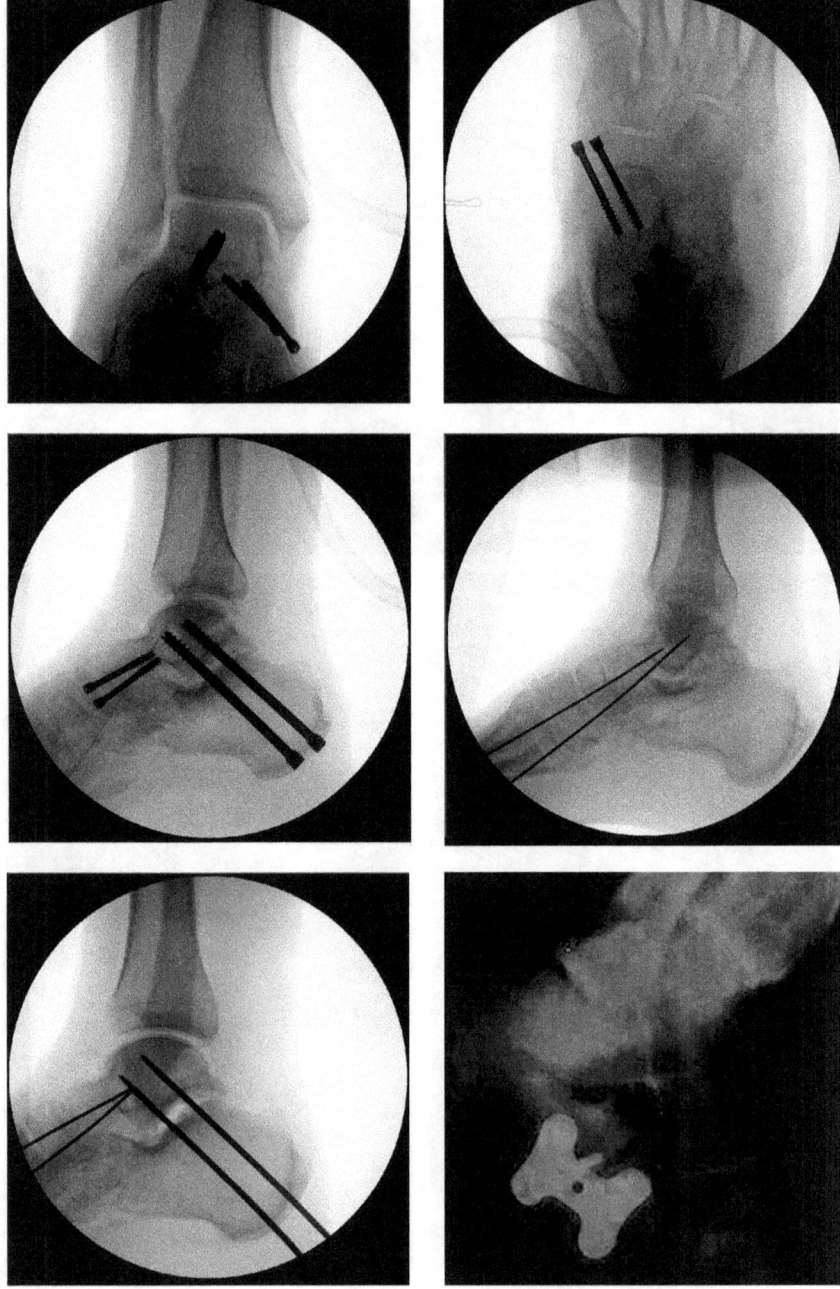

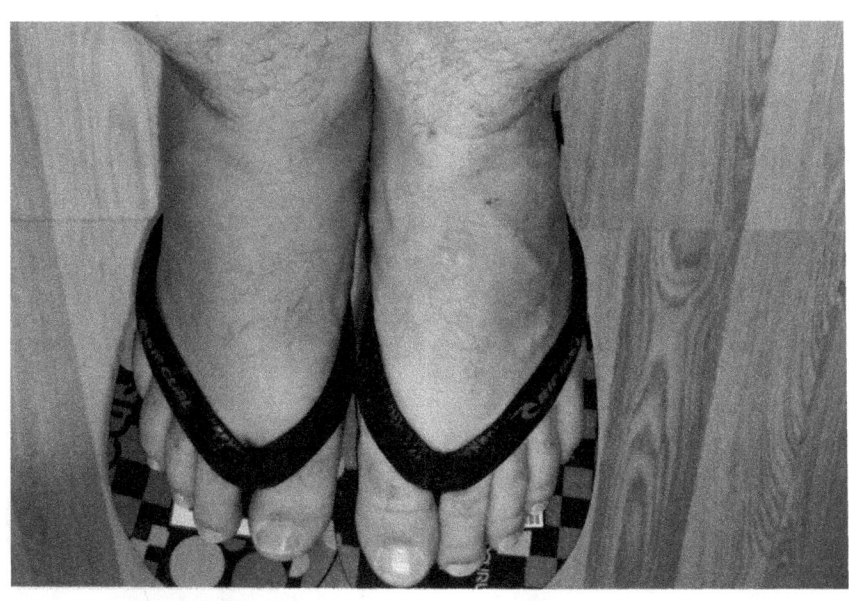
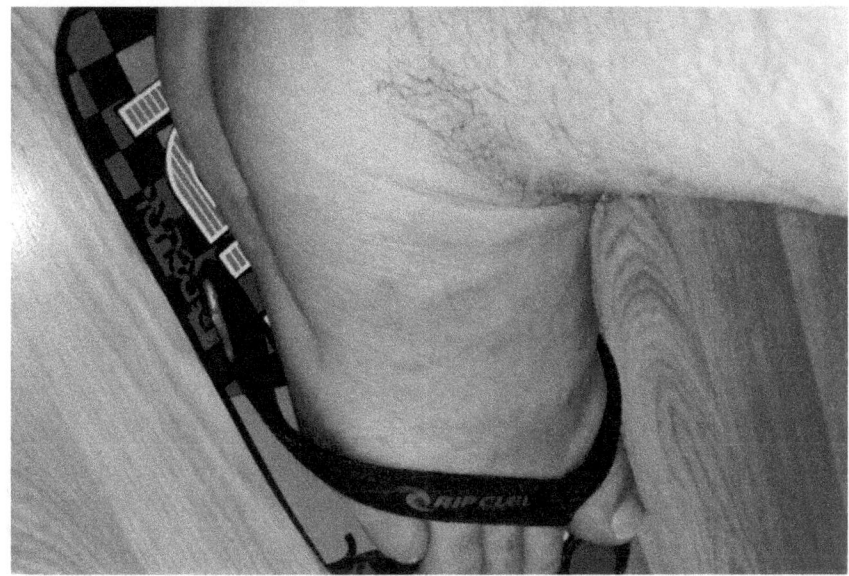

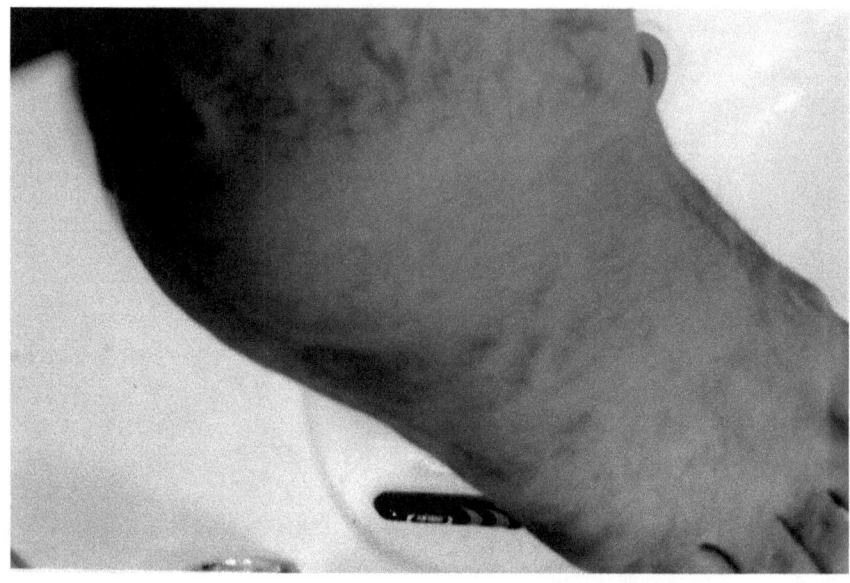
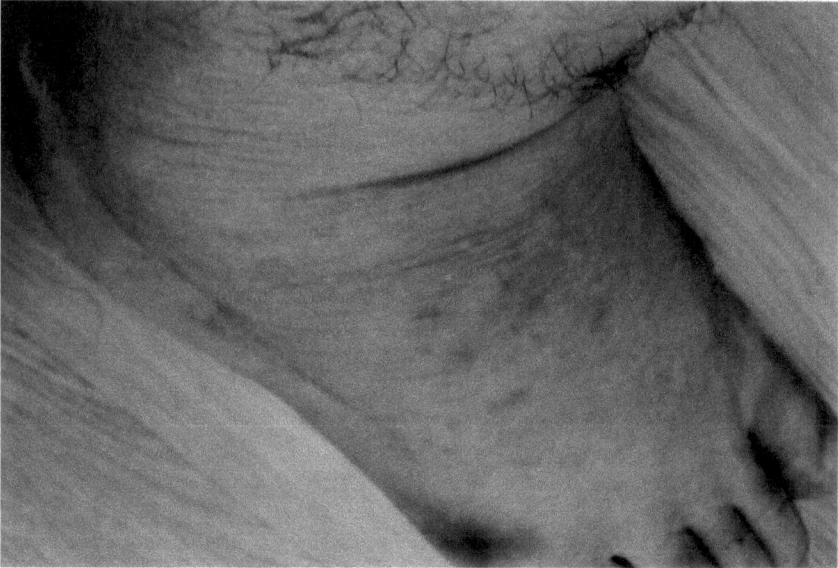

5129 / 2005

POLICE CERTIFICATE
issued by
QUEENSLAND POLICE SERVICE

This is to certify there are no 'disclosable court outcomes' recorded against the name of Jeremy Rex SMITH born in Parramatta, New South Wales on 25 July 1971 in the records of police services in Australia.

Issued at Brisbane this fourth day of April 2005.

....

Authorised Officer

Explanatory Notes

1. The person subject of this certificate has no conviction recorded by any police service in Australia or the person has incurred a conviction/s that cannot be disclosed because of legislation or police service policy applying to the conviction/s. In either case, the person has no police record to which reference can be made. There is legislation in some Australian States and Territories, and for Commonwealth offences, that provides for the non-disclosure of certain convictions after a period of time has elapsed in which the person has not been further convicted for an offence. Elsewhere, some police services apply these or other restrictions on disclosure as a matter of policy.

2. This certificate is based on a search of the name and birth particulars of the person concerned against a national reference system containing information contributed by all police services within Australia. Further reference may also have been made of the criminal records held by all or any of these police services.

3. There is a time lapse between the recording of convictions by courts and the updating of the criminal records of police services and the national reference system. This certificate only reflects the completeness and accuracy of these records and system on the date of issue.

4. The criminal records used by or available to the Queensland Police Service, in most cases, contain criminal convictions resulting from prosecutions initiated by police. Many offences are prosecuted by non-police agencies, and the details of convictions resulting from these prosecutions may not be included in this certificate. Generally, this certificate will not include traffic convictions incurred in Queensland. Such convictions are usually contained in the person's Queensland traffic history available from Queensland Transport.

1. February 2017

To whom it may concern

This is a letter of my personal opinion about Mr Jeremy Smith. I first met Jeremy when I join Conrad Jupiters Hotel (presently Jupiters casino) as Executive Pastry Chef in December 1992. He was already working at the pastry kitchen since November and he continued to work under my supervision for another 4 years till he resigned in November 1996 During this time, he was promoted to higher positions to take on more responsibilities. After he left Jupiters Hotel to start for his own business venture, we kept in touch and exchanged ideas and news about pastry and all other personal matters. Therefore, I know him not only as his supervisor chef, but also as a family friend.

During the time when we worked together 25 years ago, I was impressed with his outstanding personality. Because of his willingness to learn, it was a pleasure to train and work with him. As a result, he was also able to learn and deliver creative work under my guidance. He has proven that with a gold medal in Salon Culinaire Gold Coast at that time. We worked in a demanding environment, under high pressure, but with his time management skills, he was able to cope with the job stress and executed his duties excellently.

In general, I find Jeremy to be an honest, open-minded, and motivated worker who can be relied on to not only carry out his duties but to go the extra mile. He has shown great confidence and flair in communicating with both his subordinates and his peers. His good sense of humor makes him very likeable and approachable.

Moreover, I have always been impressed by his passion for fast cars and motorbikes. It was always enjoyable listening to him when he talks about his motor sports dreams.

I wish him all the very best for his future undertakings.

Serdar YENER
Executive Pastry Chef Conrad Jupiters (1992 – 1997)
YenersWay Cake Art Tutorials (online)
www.yenersway.com

13

PROFESSIONAL ERROR OF JUDGEMENT

17 June 2017

So finally, on the 15th December 2013 I was locked away like a caged lion inside a triple-locked door human safe-style cage in the new Gold Coast University Hospital and after, I must stress, absolutely no physical violence whatsoever, but still locked in a human style vault/cage with no way out. No daylight, no sign of human life except for the many dickheads in their *Doogie Howser* style white coats exercising their psychiatric evaluation and analysis on me. Please tell me how these people could have any idea about what was going on inside my head. But yes, believe it or not, they actually think they do, in fact how could they have any clue of what is going on inside anyone's head who is in this same position, but they believed they knew exactly. It was incredibly hard to believe that they called themselves mental health professionals, I could clearly tell that they had no professionalism about them and what I did know for sure was that they had absolutely no clue at all what they were doing. Just a bunch of clowns that had passed a university degree examination and were being paid a fortune by Australian taxpayers. It was the security guards that were doing all the work and handling all the many stressful situations and no doubt probably on way less than half the salary of the pompous dickheads in white coats, who somehow managed to call themselves doctors or mental health professionals as they preferred, it was beyond the wildest of jokes. Just keep in mind please that there was absolutely no evidence of any of the many serious allegations against me. Even Maxwell Smart's[16] secret office didn't have as many doors as my special cage did, this was simply beyond inhumane. I must note that in among this moment of lifelong disbelief the QLD police service were probably by far the most decent and easiest to deal with, but I suppose that goes without saying for a bloke with a nil criminal history. They treated me with nothing but the utmost respect and in conversation in transit they conveyed that this justice examination order was one of the most outrageous and ridiculous court orders they had ever seen and been forced to

---

16. Maxwell Smart was a fictional character in an American action spy comedy film television series called "Get Smart" that satirized the secret agent genre popular in the 1960s.

execute. I guess that was saying something, but what do you expect being legislated by an ex-military crazy powerhouse dictator by the name of Campbell Newman[17] who, quite simply in most people's minds including mine, was nothing other than a circus clown, a very wealthy circus clown and a bloke that I'd love to have my time with in the ring.

1 July 2017

The four security guards that entered my cage after I was videoing my situation for legal reasons, ended up being real true-blue top Aussie blokes. The head man asked me to try and relax and to try and keep calm, I replied, "Keep calm in an environment like this, absolutely impossible." He then asked me, "Who did this to you mate? One thing is for sure, we can tell you, based on the statistics and history of past cases year after year, it will be most definitely your wife, your mother or your sister, and that is 100%." I replied, "No doubt my hero arsehole bitch of a sister would definitely have instigated the court order, but somehow I know that my so-called wife has something to do with it as well." I said that I would like to believe that my mum wouldn't hit

---

17. Campbell Newman was the 38th premier of Queensland from 26 March 2012 to 14 February 2015.

so low, but I just knew that my spineless coward of a father, no doubt wouldn't hesitate to strike with such an incredibly low blow, because quite simply that's what cowards do, they instigate and then hibernate and basically vanish. One thing I can honestly say if I was to instigate such a low cowardly act, I would most definitely 100% execute it as well, because that's what real men do, they create, instigate and execute, they don't point a finger at the weak and the vulnerable, but these two dickheads had operated like this their entire lives, weaker than piss, I had always laughed at how weak they both were. I could only imagine the many tens of thousands being shat on like me by their so-called families and none other than the infamous QLD mental health.

The way in which this was conducted by the QLD state government was nothing short of appalling, I was given absolutely no chance whatsoever to give my version of events, just locked away with nowhere to run, stripped of every single liberty and every human right. This could only happen in the state of QLD, not in any of the other states in Australia. Their mental health laws were set up in a more civil manner and legislated in a much more humane way, their patients were shown decency and respect and did get to give their complete versions of events, but when you've got more than one ganging up against you through brainwash and much manipulation, well, you are pretty well screwed. Extremely hard for me still to comprehend that a disabled man who just wanted to pursue a lifelong dream and to speak of the cold hard facts and truth about child sex abuse, should go through more abuse, but as we all know my failed parents who, in many ways, especially in respect of myself, had neglected their three children, simply didn't like hearing the truth, and because of that I paid the ultimate price. Carpet sweepers I prefer to call them.

25 July 2017

Here are some of the notes which the Dr Haritha Devineni team fabricated against me, some of it absolutely true, much of it completely false, and what intrigues me is that they were silly enough to put perjury into black and white. I had never been outsmarted, and I wasn't about to start now with government doctors' fabrications and deceit purely to protect their own arses, because the mental health clowns in the court had chosen to believe a pathological liar, a man who thrived on power and the constant self-aggrandisement but who, quite honestly in most people's eyes, was nothing other than a human failure in more ways than one.

It is truly sad when your own 14-year-old daughter has

Jeremy Smith

Clinical Report - ITO Review for SMITH, Jeremy on 15/01/2014 at 12:00 PM

Clinical report
involuntary treatment order review

Mental Health Review Tribunal

NOTE: THIS REPORT IS TO BE RECEIVED BY THE TRIBUNAL ONE WEEK BEFORE THE DATE OF THE REVIEW

Patient's details	Hearing Date: 22/01/2014
Given name/s: Jeremy	Family name: SMITH
Date of birth: 25/07/1971	Record No. 221062

	Involuntary status
Treating service	Authorised mental health service: GCMHS
	☑ Involuntary treatment order specify ☐ In-patient category
	Date made: 15/12/2013 ☑ Community category
More than one may apply	☐ Classified patient and/or ☐ Court order (s101(2), 273(1)(b), 337(5)) specify .... In Prison ☐ Yes ☐ No
Patient's location	
	Attendance at hearing
	Will the patient be attending the hearing? ☑ Yes ☐ No ☐ Not Sure
	Is the patient currently Absent without Permission? ☐ Yes ☐ No
	If yes, date of last contact with the AMHS ....
Give details of any other action taken for the patient's return	Authority to Return Issued ☐ Yes ☐ No If yes, date issued ....
Insert date *if applicable*	**Patient access to report**
	The full contents of the report and attachments has been discussed with the patient on: 20/01/2014
	and/or
	A copy of the report and attachments has been provided in full to the patient on: 20/01/2014
	An application for a Confidentiality Order has been made ☐ Yes ☐ No
Please annex: • Treatment Plan • any relevant reports from other members of the treating team	**Documents annexed** List documents annexed

First signed by: DEVINENI, Haritha	Discipline: Medical Officer Specialist - Psychiatrist/Consultant Psychiatrist	Date: 16/01/2014	Time: 9:04 AM
	Note: This document has been signed 1 time(s). Multiple signatures will be listed on the last page where applicable. Electronically signed documents within CIMHA form only part of the consumer's complete clinical record		

Consumer ID:415240   PDF Ref No:299161

Clinical Report - ITO Review for SMITH, Jeremy on 15/01/2014 at 12:00 PM

Treating team

Consultant Psychiatrist	Name: Dr Devineni		
Case Manager	Name: Nick Blythe	Employment Category:	
Registrar/Medical Officer	Name: Dr R. Balasubramaniam		
Other	Name:		

Current diagnosis of mental illness

Diagnosis

Provisional/differential diagnoses

Bipolar affective disorder

History of Mental Illness

Include relevant dates, description and circumstances of symptoms observed, and treatment progress; history of willingness to undertake treatment

Background:

Jeremy Smith is a 42 male, who works as a pastry chef and lives with his wife (Vanessa) and children in a rental accommodation in a rental accommodation in Mermaid Waters. Jeremy was previously diagnosed with clinical depression and was treated on Desvenlafaxine, with maximum dose of 200mg once daily, which was gradually weaned down with a view to cessation as Jeremy was exhibiting signs of a hypomanic episode. Jeremy was also commenced on Ziprasidone as a mood stabiliser which was later ceased. Prior to the hospital admission, Jeremy's presentation was in keeping with that of hypomania, diagnosis was revised to Bipolar Affective Disorder by Dr Lichter (Private Psychiatrist) and he was commenced on low dose Quetiapine for mania with a view to increase the dose in an attempt to optimise his medications in the community.

Admission to Robina Hospital Acute Adult Mental Health Ward (15.12.2013 – 06.01.2014)

Diagnosis: Bipolar Affective Disorder

Jeremy was reviewed by Acute Care Team at home following the initiation of a JEO by a family member. Main concerns listed on the JEO included a recent diagnosis of BPAD by his private psychiatrist, with lack of engagement on Jeremy's part as he failed to attend a follow-up appointment. There were reports that Jeremy was driving dangerously and recklessly and was involved in a motor vehicle accident with one of his children. He has boasted to family members that he reached speeds of 240km/hr fish tailed for 600m and entered a corner at 140km/hr. Jeremy had purchased a V8 Super Car and had plans to take up race car driving and was hoping to gain sponsorship from Jerry Harvey. He was reported to have been argumentative and had taken two family members on drives and had exceeded speeds of 170km/hr. In response to the JEO, Jeremy was reviewed by the ACT clinician who expressed concerns for Jeremy as he was experiencing a manic episode; Jeremy had displayed "pressured speech, flight of ideas and at times loosening of associations, delusions of grandiosity…".

First signed by: DEVINENI, Haritha	Discipline: Medical Officer Specialist - Psychiatrist/Consultant Psychiatrist	Date: 16/01/2014	Time: 9:04 AM

Note: This document has been signed 1 time(s). Multiple signatures will be listed on the last page where applicable.
Electronically signed documents within CIMHA form only part of the consumer's complete clinical record

Consumer ID: 415240	PDF Ref No: 299181

Jeremy Smith

Clinical Report - ITO Review for SMITH, Jeremy on 15/01/2014 at 12:00 PM

Jeremy was advised that further assessment and management in the community was warranted to optimise his medications.

Jeremy was initially agreeable to follow-up with the ACT in the community, however, the team received a phone call from Vanessa who reported that Jeremy informed her that he would not attend clinic appointment. Jeremy was described as being elevated, was threating legal action against the Acute Care Team and left their residence and did not return home. Jeremy then contacted ACT and reported that he had an appointment scheduled and advised the clinician that he would not attend. He advised the clinician that if QLD Health contacts him again, he will launch legal action and informed staff that he had already consulted solicitors and a barrister. He informed the clinician about his prejudicial upbringing and indicated that he suffered from depression as a result of this; he spoke about the diagnosis of BPAD and informed the clinician that he strongly disagreed with this. Further phone calls were made by Vanessa, expressing ongoing concerns for the patient. She confirmed that Jeremy had been driving erratically and dangerously and was involved in an accident while his daughter was in the passenger seat. Vanessa also expressed concerns as Jeremy had contacted her "demanding" that he have his sons ready at 15:30hours so that he can take them to O'Reilly's at Mount Tambourine for a drive. Vanessa expressed concerns over her sons' safety as a result of Jeremy's erratic behaviour and reckless driving. Due to these concerns, Vanessa decided to go and stay in Byron Bay with Jeremy's parents and did not answer his phone calls. Vanessa also informed the ACT clinician that Jeremy threatened to call the police because she had taken the children over the border. In light of this, Jeremy was commenced on a Request for Assessment and Recommendation for Assessment.

Jeremy was reviewed by the psychiatry registrar on-duty – during the review, Jeremy reported experiencing clinical depression following a broken bone in his foot and had become house bound following this. He reported a recent diagnosis of BPAD and reported that the dose of Desvenlafaxine was reduced; however Jeremy was not compliant with the dose reduction and was taking a higher dose of Desvenlafaxine. He "discussed at length his superior knowledge of orthopaedics, and that the surgeons were amazed with his intellect following the repair of his fracture". Reports from the review noted that, "it was difficult to keep Jeremy on topic during the interview" and Jeremy had reported problems with anger at home. He admitted to driving more than 175km/hr multiple times over four days. He denied problems with his behaviour and stated that he was a male and that's what they do to blow off steam. Jeremy reported feeling the best he has ever felt and denied thoughts of self-harm and thoughts of harming others. Collateral from his mother-in-law revealed that Jeremy had made a phone call at 4.40am and did not make sense during the discussion. The content of the discussion included his intended legal actions against his sister over the JEO. His mother-in-law acknowledged Vanessa's concerns for their children if Jeremy was to drive at high speeds. His mother-in-law did not believe that he would intentionally harm his children but acknowledged the possibility of harm by misadventure if he were to drive recklessly. Following the assessment by the on-duty psychiatry registrar, it was decided that an admission was warranted for longitudinal assessment, containment of risks and for initiation of treatment for mania.

Jeremy was admitted under the care of Dr Devineni (Consultant psychiatrist) and was

First signed by: DEVINENI, Haritha	Discipline: Medical Officer Specialist - Psychiatrist/Consultant Psychiatrist	Date: 15/01/2014	Time: 9:04 AM
	Note: This document has been signed 1 time(s). Multiple signatures will be listed on the last page where applicable. Electronically signed documents within CIMHA form only part of the consumer's complete clinical record		
Consumer ID:415240	PDF Ref No:299181		

Clinical Report - ITO Review for SMITH, Jeremy on 15/01/2014 at 12:00 PM

reviewed following admission. He presented as manic, with circumstantial thought form with over-inclusion of ideas during the conversation. During the interview, the topic of his childhood dreams with regards to undertaking a V8 race in Bathurst was explored and Jeremy and his friend reported that it was just a "dream" that he had shared with some friends; Jeremy also disclosed his own childhood molestation perpetrated by paternal grandfather. Jeremy also discussed his family dynamics and told the team that his aunt had taken a large amount of money of the family's inheritance in a scrupulous manner and informed the team that the sum of money was given to his aunt to convince her to cover-up the story about Jeremy's childhood molestation. Following a period of longitudinal assessment, the team was in agreement with previous assessments in the community that Jeremy was undergoing a manic episode. The Quetiapine was increased to 100mg at night, and the dose was gradually increased by 100mg a day. Jeremy was established on 300mg of Quetiapine twice daily, but complained of increased sedation with orthostatic hypotension. As a result of this, the Quetiapine was changed to 400mg twice daily and was administered as a slow release. Jeremy still complained of side-effects. Following subsequent reviews, Jeremy still displayed limited insight into his mental illness and stated that his condition will worsen in the hospital environment. He expressed the desire to appeal against the ITO. Jeremy was advised that hospital admission is warranted and became increasingly agitated. He asked the consultant, "is your indemnity in order?" and stated that criminal lawyers could become involved if he continued to be an inpatient. She then asked if Queensland Health will pay $600 a day for the loss of income. Collateral from nursing staff revealed that there were some "litigious ideas evident about prosecuting QLD Health for loss of pay, and his family for placing him under the MHA". He told nursing staff that he has criminal lawyers on the case and that he "will win". For the purpose of treating Jeremy in the least restricted way, he was given graduated leave with family. Collateral reports that he was irritable and was verbally abusive towards his family. Given his level of agitation, irritability and high absconsion risk, he was transferred to PICU for further management in a low stimulus environment. Following transfer from PICU, Jeremy remained irritable. The team believed that the Seroquel did not give the desired therapeutic effect and Jeremy was complaining of side-effect. In light of this, the Seroquel was ceased and Jeremy was established on Olanzapine 5mg in the morning and 15mg at night. Following transfer, he was described as "unsettled" on occasions. Jeremy tried to request for leave and his behaviour was described as "escalating" by the nursing staff; he was "annoyed with delays". Clonazepam was started for a brief period of time to lower his level of agitation and was gradually weaned and ceased. Following the commencement of Olanzapine, Jeremy appeared to have been more settled, and was given graduated leave which he utilised with good effect. He still expressed discontent regarding the hospital admission.

He was reviewed by Dr Paul Rogers (Consultant psychiatrist) who also agreed that Jeremy had experienced a manic episode which was in the process of remitting. Jeremy was discharged home on Olanzapine 5mg in the morning and 15mg at night. He was discharged on a community-category ITO for a period of stabilisation in the community.

First signed by: DEVINENI, Haritha	Discipline: Medical Officer Specialist - Psychiatrist/Consultant Psychiatrist	Date: 16/01/2014	Time: 9:04 AM
	Note: This document has been signed 1 time(s). Multiple signatures will be listed on the last page where applicable. Electronically signed documents within CIMHA form only part of the consumer's complete clinical record		
Consumer ID:415240	PDF Ref No:299161		

Jeremy Smith

Clinical Report - ITO Review for SMITH, Jeremy on 15/01/2014 at 12:00 PM

Significant events and precipitating factors leading to making of the ITO	**Circumstances leading to the Involuntary Treatment Order** Please refer to the above section.
Provide details of the patient's CURRENT mental state.	**Current mental state assessment** For the purposes of this report, the patient/client was last examined by the ☐ psychiatrist ☑ doctor ☐ case manager (tick one) on 14/01/2014 If not the psychiatrist above, please note the date on which the patient was last examined by a psychiatrist 06/01/2014 Caucasian male appearing of stated age, reasonably kempt wearing casual attire. Superficial rapport established and patient was cooperative during the interview. Appropriate eye contact throughout the interview. No psychomotor disturbances were observed. Speech was of increased rate (not pressured), increased volume with normal inflection of tone. Mood objectively euthymic. Normal range and reactivity of affect. Thought was circumstantial and tangential with overinclusion of ideas. Thought was focused on his mental state since hospital discharge, his day structures, goals and plans for the future. Circumstances that led to the hospital admission was also revisited and discussed at length. Perceptual disturbances were not explored. Insight - limited; while Jeremy agreed that he had a mental illness, he reports that he suffers from Depression rather than BPAD; he did not acknowledged that he had experienced a manic episode and instead stated that he was "angry" and thought that his wife and other members of the family had taken things out of proportion and acknowledged that this was the reason for his hospital admission. Judgement - partial as Jeremy superficially agrees to comply with medications and agreed to present to Palm Beach Clinic.
	Informed Consent (a) Is the patient capable of giving informed consent to the treatment? ☐ Yes ☑ No The most recent assessment of capacity to consent was made on: 14/01/2014 (b) If yes above, has the patient unreasonably refused the proposed treatment? ☑ Yes ☐ No While Jeremy agrees that he previously suffered from depression and was in remission; there is still disagreement with the diagnosis of BPAD. Of note, Jeremy failed to attend his follow-up appointment with Dr Lichter for review of medications and failed to attend the community appointment with ACT. Jeremy remains discontent with the hospital admission and has been documented to have made verbal threats with regards to taking legal action against QLD Health, his treating consultant and the MHA.

First signed by:	Discipline:	Date:	Time:
DEVINENI, Haritha	Medical Officer Specialist - Psychiatrist/Consultant Psychiatrist	16/01/2014	9:04 AM

Note: This document has been signed 1 time(s). Multiple signatures will be listed on the last page where applicable. Electronically signed documents within CIMHA form only part of the consumer's complete clinical record

Consumer ID:415240   PDF Ref No:299161

Clinical Report - ITO Review for SMITH, Jeremy on 15/01/2014 at 12:00 PM

Specify -	**Risk Issues**
	(a) Risk to self
• nature of risk • relevant dates • past incidences • reasons for concern	Jeremy's risk of self harm through misadventure is moderate in the short to medium term. If he were to experience a deterioration in mental state, he would continue to drive in a precarious manner endangering his own life and the lives of his children if they were to remain in the care while he drove at high speeds. His risk of suicide is low in the short to medium term. Of note, Jeremy has not made any suicide attempts and did not report suicidal ideation to the multidisciplinary team. Jeremy's main risk is that of a serious deterioration in his mental state should he become non-compliant with medical treatment. Of note, Jeremy was advised to reduce the dose of Desvenlafaxine by his private psychiatrist to avoid the possibility of an antidepressant-induced mania. However, Jeremy continued to take the dose that was higher than the recommended prescription and had failed to attend a follow-up appointment. Following review by the ACT clinician, Jeremy was also advised to attend a clinic appointment with a psychiatrist for review of medications to avoid hospital admission; he neglected to engage with ACT in the community. Jeremy has refused to engage with the community treatment team and has not adhered to the treatment plan devised by his private psychiatrist. (b) Risk to others Due to his reckless driving, Jeremy is at risk of harming others if he was to sustain a motor vehicle accident. Of note, he was reported to have taken two family members on drives and had exceeded speeds of 170km/hr. He has also boasted to family members that he reached speeds of 240km/hr fish tailed for 800m and entered a corner at 140km/hr. Jeremy also admitted to driving more than 175km/hr multiple times over four days when he was reviewed by the admitting psychiatry registrar. These concerns were significant to the extent that it has been raised to the multidisciplinary team by various members of the family. Jeremy has also made verbal threats to the multidisciplinary team informing them that he would be taking legal action against QLD health, the treating team and the MHA. Jeremy has not been physically aggressive on the ward. There are no significant forensic issues to date.
Provide details of:	**Current treatment**
• the current medication • the patient's progress and response to involuntary treatment • treatment plan and/or annex the treatment plan • treatment plan implementation issues	Olanzapine 5mg in the morning and 15mg at night

First signed by:	Discipline:	Date:	Time:
DEVINENI, Haritha	Medical Officer Specialist - Psychiatrist/Consultant Psychiatrist	16/01/2014	9:04 AM

Note: This document has been signed 1 time(s). Multiple signatures will be listed on the last page where applicable.
Electronically signed documents within CIMHA form only part of the consumer's complete clinical record

Consumer ID:415240   PDF Ref No:299161

Jeremy Smith

Clinical Report - ITO Review for SMITH, Jeremy on 15/01/2014 at 12:00 PM

Social circumstances report
Social Networks and the Capacity to Support the Patient

Provide details of risks and protective factors in the patients social environment eg:
- carer and other significant relationships
- carers capacity to support the patient

Jeremy lives with a supportive wife and three children. He has a childhood friend Dave who has also been supportive of Jeremy during his inpatient stay. Since the hospital admission, Jeremy has not made any contacts with his sister. He has also isolated himself from his extended family as he has not come to terms with the circumstances in which the JEO has been taken and has ongoing conflict with his father regarding the lack of social support when he divulged his childhood molestation with his family.

Accommodation

Provide details of:
- the arrangements in place for where the patient will live

Jeremy is currently living in a rental accommodation in Mermaid Waters.

Financial Affairs
Does the patient have a substitute decision-maker for financial matters? ☐ Yes ☒ No

Use of Time

Comment on:
- how the patient uses his/her day
- employment and/or other activities

He works 30 hours/week as a pastry chef. He enjoys spending his time with his children, going to the beach, watching the cricket. Jeremy still has passion for motor sports and still has dreams with regards to Bathurst. He has goals to financially stabilise himself.

Aboriginal and Torres Strait Islander patients
Cultural information to be completed by the treating team
! For patients from other culturally & linguistically diverse backgrounds please use the *Patient cultural and language considerations* report form

(a) Cultural background
☐ Aboriginal ☐ Torres Strait islander ☐ Both Aboriginal and Torres Strait Islander

(b) Communication/language interpreter required
☐ Yes *specify language* ☐ No

(c) Will a Cultural support person be attending the hearing?
☐ Yes ☐ No

Provide details of:
Cultural background (e.g. clan group, languages spoken, community of origin)

First signed by:	Discipline:	Date:	Time:
DEVINENI, Haritha	Medical Officer Specialist - Psychiatrist/Consultant Psychiatrist	16/01/2014	9:04 AM

Note: This document has been signed 1 time(s). Multiple signatures will be listed on the last page where applicable. Electronically signed documents within CIMHA form only part of the consumer's complete clinical record

Consumer ID:415240 PDF Ref No:299181

Supercharged Goosebumps 2481

Clinical Report - ITO Review for SMITH, Jeremy on 15/01/2014 at 12:00 PM

Community (e.g. networks, engagement and acceptance by the community, community supports and how these are contributing to the patient's recovery)

Family background (e.g. family dynamic, kinship, cultural adoption, issues relating to stolen generation, grief and loss)

Cultural issues impacting on treatment (e.g. need for an interpreter, spiritual beliefs, gender issues, payback)

Cultural support being provided (e.g. IMHW, cultural support worker, community organisations)

Cultural information completed by

Print Name:
Position:
Date:

Recommendation/Reasons

If recommending that the Involuntary Treatment Order continue -

(a) specify why involuntary treatment is currently required and the likely risks if the patient were not on an ITO

While Jeremy agrees that he has been diagnosed with clinical depression previously, he still failed to acknowledge the diagnosis of BPAD. He has disengaged with ACT and has been lost to follow-up with his private psychiatrist. Jeremy still expressed his discontent with regards to the circumstances that led to the hospital admission, and remains vexatious with regards to inpatient management. His risk of non-compliance with medication and disengagement with the treatment team is significant. If he were to become non-compliant with medications, take incorrect doses and disengage with the treatment team, there would be a serious deterioration in mental state that will exacerbate the risks outlined above, including his risk to himself and risk to others.

(b) specify reasons why the patients mental health and wellbeing cannot be adequately promoted and maintained with any less restrictive treatment (for inpatients, why is a community category of order not currently appropriate?)

We have previously attempted to treat Jeremy in the least restrictive way, as a voluntary patient in the community. Jeremy has taken his medications at dosages that were not prescribed and was loss to follow-up with his private psychiatrist and has suffered from a deterioration in mental state as a result of this. A community category ITO would present as the least restrictive way to manage Jeremy in the community without compromising his mental state. We will continue to evaluate his need for treatment on an involuntary basis.

Report MUST be signed by the treating psychiatrist

Declaration

Report prepared by   Approved by

First signed by: DEVINENI, Haritha	Discipline: Medical Officer Specialist - Psychiatrist/Consultant Psychiatrist	Date: 15/01/2014	Time: 9:04 AM

Note: This document has been signed 1 time(s). Multiple signatures will be listed on the last page where applicable. Electronically signed documents within CIMHA form only part of the consumer's complete clinical record

Consumer ID:415240   PDF Ref No:299161

Jeremy Smith

Clinical Report - ITO Review for SMITH, Jeremy on 15/01/2014 at 12:00 PM

If the person preparing the report is not the treating psychiatrist for the patient	Signature	Signature
	Print Name Dr Renuka Balasubramaniam	Print Name Dr Devineni
	Designation PHO - Psychiatry	Treating Psychiatrist Dr Devineni
	Date 15/01/2014	Date 15/01/2014

To: **Mental Health Review Tribunal**
PO Box 15818 City East, Brisbane QLD 4002

First signed by: DEVINENI, Haritha
Discipline: Medical Officer Specialist - Psychiatrist/Consultant Psychiatrist
Date: 16/01/2014 Time: 9:04 AM

Note: This document has been signed 1 time(s). Multiple signatures will be listed on the last page where applicable. Electronically signed documents within CIMHA form only part of the consumer's complete clinical record

Consumer ID:415240   PDF Ref No:299161

to come clean with the truth about what was said about me in the Southport Magistrates Court; in my book a 14-year-old child should never be allowed anywhere near a court of law. A young child that was pressured and placed in a bad position and from nothing other than pure fear and intimidation forced into agreeing with everything that the fuckwit Rex Smith said, a man that simply had never had any balls and was nothing other than a limp dick human being. And believe me, more than every second person I know thought the same, including many family members, but they simply didn't have the guts to say it. I had told him many times to his face, and like many of my lifelong mates had said, this was purely payback, I guess the truth did really hurt indeed.

In summary reading through the report myself many times over and over, trying to make sense of the many fabrications, I must say I find it both hilarious and at the same time extremely disturbing. The biggest thing was how could these people make such serious allegations and accusations about me when they had only known me for 21 days? Most people were of the same inclination; how could they make an assessment based mostly on what they had been told by others, most of which was blatant lies? When I put them on the spot – family members I mean – most were back-pedalling quicker than any of them had ever run forward in their entire lives. This QLD mental health report with its firm allegations and many accusations and the intensity of its perjury was probably a document that was just going to lead to a public disaster and public outrage. Many lawyers I spoke with said it was one of the most badly written documents that they had ever set eyes on. I must say I still laugh almost four years on at the so-called fishtails I did at 240 kilometres per hour, I would certainly love to see that. But the real cracker was that I had purchased a V8 supercar, which had a dollar value of approximately AUD$600,000 dollars. My actual Holden Commodore V8 was a little different, it was worth a mere AUD$30,000, just the slightest of difference in price tags and the car itself.

Also it must be noted that on page 6 of 9 of the clinical report, it states clearly that "Jeremy has not been physically aggressive on the ward", however, I have in my possession a 143-page report that suggests very differently and that, in fact, I was very physically aggressive. This report was fabricated many years later, some three years later to be accurate, after the initial clinical discharge report had been written. Amusing how things took a sudden change in direction as I requested all relevant documents through Freedom of Information. These people were simply nothing other than circus clowns, and I prefer to refer to them as human scum, together with Rex Smith and Karen Justice at the very top of the list titled "Human Scumbags".

These people, the doctors I mean, conducted themselves in exactly the same way as did Karen Justice and Rex Smith, they simply backed each other 100% so that there was never a chance of being wrong but, in fact, they were. There was never a diagnosis of bipolar affective disorder from my private psychiatrist, they had simply made it all up and it was fabricated purely to protect all QLD government officials involved, including, and especially, the Southport Magistrates Court.

8 August 2017

I mean after all who would ever have believed two family members, who both had histories of putting people into mental institutions – my mum by Rex Smith, four years on and off in Richmond Clinic, and one of my many brothers-in-law, Kevin, by Karen Justice into a mental institution in Currumbin on the Gold Coast for three months. This deranged woman also put an innocent music teacher from Byron Bay Primary School through an excessive amount of sheer hell, suggesting that her young son Adam was being sexually interfered with by this super friendly, nice bloke music teacher. The authorities started believing her without understanding her obscure, delusional and obsessively deranged thought patterns, but it was very clear to me that she simply was a man hater. These two family members, Rex and Karen, are both serial narcissistic sociopaths who thrive on power and manipulation, and they have turned everything back onto the people who they had chronically abused and done wrong by. This super bitch, Karen Justice, institutionalised her second husband into a mental facility while she was off jet-setting and committing adultery, but hey, remember she was nothing but a saint, believe me when I say on behalf of many ex-husbands she was anything but. This low-life human being was doused with evil. This was a woman who just couldn't mind her own business; her judgemental personality and the way in which she conducted her life, but mostly others' lives, was nothing short of an appalling disgrace, she abused women's rights like I had never seen before. What she needed to do, along with the cowardly Rex Smith, was to turn the clipboard on themselves and take a good hard look in the mirror and just accept that they were honestly just two nobodies who had lied their way through life, something that my mother had taught me not to do. I guess their power obsessions came from the fact that they were both extremely insecure and most of all, incredibly piss weak, both had failed at whatever career path they had ever chosen. One being nothing other than a Band-Aid nurse that didn't last, a failed small business owner that blamed her second husband for everything including cash theft, and now an online dog biscuit entrepreneur that had turned a "lemon into a 10-million dollar empire", just another vicious lie. And Rex, oh you must laugh, a man who ordered beer and dusted wine bottles for 35 years on a bare minimum wage, who told everyone who came into his company that he knew more about money than anyone he had ever come across, and in his deranged mind he actually believed he was solely responsible for his long-term employer's wealth, he couldn't have been further from the truth. The failure of his past land development left him with extremely abusive baggage that he just couldn't seem to shrug off. Of all the stories I had heard over the many years, this one made me constantly laugh to myself; he knew more about money than anyone, purely he thought from being a banker wanker, but the funny thing was, he had none. I would laugh uncontrollably with many family and non-family members over his weird and delusional mentality, it simply was dead set hilarious. He demanded constant attention when he was diagnosed with diabetes type II; while I suffered the pain and personal heartache of my crushed foot injury over many years with surgery after surgery he insisted that he knew how crippling my pain was as he had injured an Achilles tendon. My Achilles tendon was also buggered, but compared to the many other forms of pain throughout my foot I can honestly say that I'd had splinters that hurt more than my Achilles, but he continued to ramble that his tendon pain was similar to that of my right foot crush injury. He was one of these dickheads who simply believed that anything you can do, I can do better. He thrived on and needed constant attention, as did his deranged daughter, while all I wanted was for my pain to go away and to be able to walk unaided, but this just wasn't to be. I hated any form of attention, including having a simple photo taken, and had my entire life. So, although I loved winning everything and anything, especially in sport, I had always disliked accolades in every sense and form. This undoubtedly was a trait deeply inherited from my mum; I was very much my mother's son, and she had that funny Scottish fire in her as did I, although mine was more of a volcanic loaded TNT explosion in my persona, but only if you pissed and shat on me in a big way, of which to date so many had. And I believe that was purely because of my overly generous nature towards helping others, some purely grateful, but most not so, the 80–20 principle applied to this as well, one thing for sure though was that unlike my mum, I would never be controlled, manipulated, abused and most of all, severely brainwashed.

So, after an extensive investigation of my own of not less than 3 ½ years with a select group of private mental health professionals, I began to learn that I had never suffered from the critical mental illness of bipolar affective disorder, just extreme anxiety. And coupled with my life-changing injury, depression as a result of 24/7 levels of chronic excruciating and debilitating pain, something many had absolutely no idea about, but one thing was for sure, everyone was an expert when it came to judging me, this was the one thing that was certain. I mean really was it any wonder that I suffered from these medical conditions, abused and neglected equally at an extreme level, especially as a young child and teenager, starting from the age of only 6 ½ years old.

I, and many private mental health professionals, strongly suggest that as a so-called father, Rex Stanley Smith was as bad or quite possibly worse than the abusers themselves, after all he himself was one of the biggest and best ever abusers still standing. So, I suppose it goes beyond question of doubt he was just a true born coward just like the rest of the spineless arseholes. He abused mainly me and my mum and only anyone weaker than himself, this man was a true version of an incredibly weak human being, a so-called man, someone you simply just didn't want as a father; many counsellors suggested that both he and his daughter Karen Justice were both serial narcissistic sociopaths, and after my personal four years of study I suggest that both are of the same pernicious nature, mentality and personality. I also learned from my private specialists, my study and my general practitioner of 26 years, Dr Dennis McMahon, that these types of human beings always work in pairs.

5 October 2017

This conflictive and inflictive 21-day diagnosis from Dr Haritha Devineni and her spineless so-called mental health team of the infamous bipolar affective disorder (BPAD) was made and given to me for no reason other than political gain of every part of the mental health legislation of Queensland. The Southport courthouse and the mental health ward of the Robina Hospital had completely screwed it up yet again, something I was familiar with already over the many misdiagnosed conditions of my right foot and ankle injury, it just confirmed to me that doctors aren't always right; in fact through my own personal experience they were, in fact, wrong more times than they were right. For me there wasn't a great deal of any kind of diagnosis that the Robina Hospital and their so-called doctors had managed to get right, I most certainly would never forget the so many wrongs.

I mean, after all, diagnosing someone with BPAD just because they are threatening to sue is nothing short of not only professional negligence, but the highest level of extreme medical negligence. Isn't that what they have medical indemnity insurance for, after all? But the real truth is they didn't want to be challenged legally, and as I quickly discovered, a bipolar affective disorder diagnosis would quickly eliminate the possibility of that happening. I find that to be purely gutless and spineless, just a government doctor using and abusing her power, no doubt as she did to many hundreds, even thousands, not just me. But quite simply Dr Haritha Devineni was a female version of Dr Jayant Patel[18], and I and many others would suggest she should be struck off the Australian Medical Board, with her many Indian counterparts from the Robina Hospital as she would most definitely be more suited back in her third-world country of birth, India. I mean we all know doctors and especially many so-called specialists, screw it up on a daily basis, but based on my personal experience, I would strongly suggest that the particular Indian team members in charge of the mental health ward at the Robina Hospital, Queensland, would be more suited as taxi drivers, call centre operators or perhaps more qualified to be shopping trolley collectors, with an opportunity to even drive a tractor. They were most certainly not mental health doctors, in fact, they preferred to call themselves psychiatrists, but at least my private psychiatrist

---

18. Jayant Mukundray Patel is an Indian-born American surgeon who was accused of gross negligence whilst working at Bundaberg Base Hospital in Queensland, Australia. Deaths of some of Patel's patients led to widespread publicity in 2005. Wikipedia. https://en.wikipedia.org/wiki/Jayant_Patel [Accessed: 12 May 2019]

had always been open and extremely honest with me at all times. He agreed too that the diagnosis of BPAD was quite likely given to avoid any form of litigation, but after all if they screwed it up – which they do on a day to day basis – they should be made to suffer the consequences accordingly, but instead lifelong changing consequences were placed upon me. These people should have been made accountable for the chronic health conditions that they would leave me battling with for the following four years. They had given me major endocrine difficulties and were 110% responsible for my massive major nervous breakdown together with Rex Smith and Karen 'no joy' Justice. Believe me when I say there was absolutely nothing healthy about my experience with Queensland mental health. I was just a human being who had been through an incredibly trying time from October 2008 until December of 2017 with a life-changing injury, not being able to walk as I had for the first 35 years of my life, so for me it was a pretty major ordeal. I had always maintained more energy than the Energiser bunny, but was forced to slow down to that of a garden snail doused with Yates Snail pellets – this, in fact, was how I referred to myself trying to move forward with my life in the best possible way I could. The other significant thing was that I had been hanging onto to a 35-year-old secret of being sexually abused, almost daily by the sickening, disgusting, skin-crawling paedophile Frederick Stanley Smith; I was imploding majorly with absolutely no way of knowing how to cope with the problem as it decided to surface. This was a whole new form of emotional discharge for me and an incredibly complicated thing for me to digest comprehensively; this was a tidal wave of emotions and a psychological supercharged typhoon that gobbled me up and spat me back out, this together with trying so hard to walk again riddled with severe, chronic, excruciating and crippling pain, was just too much, and on top of this a man pestering and harassing me for money... yes, I just couldn't comprehend how this was all taking place.

The so-called money expert Rex Smith was constantly pressuring me for AUD$5,000 to pay off his credit card, and was demanding this money at an interest rate of 7%; this added pressure was a major contribution to sending me into a flat spin, because after all, this clown had never lent me one cent. It came to me as a massive shock, I had just lost my house and family home, was bankrupt and facing the toughest time of my life health wise, and this fuckwit was creating the same situation as the many different lotto winners and their friends who had their hands out. So did Rex Smith, but this was perfectly normal for a human being who only had his best interests at heart, no one else's, and to make matters even worse he then completely denied it when I confronted him in front of my mother and my good mate Gilly, "Why," I said, "did you ask me for that money when you had absolutely no way of being able to pay it back?" He blatantly replied, "I never asked you for the money, you offered the money to me so I could pay off our credit card." I was flabbergasted, but here he was twisting and turning things yet again, just as his deranged daughter did to many different people as well. I mean, after all, who offers to pay off somebody's credit card? To date I've never yet heard of anyone offering to pay off someone else's credit card. The master of lies and manipulation was at it again, it was at this stage I decided to completely disown my parents, I just couldn't believe the lie after lie even though I was in a very poor state of mind from being locked in cages thanks to Queensland mental health and the infamous Karen 'no joy' Justice and Rex Stanley Smith – and my stupid naïve mother still believed all of this man's lies and deceit; I felt like leaning across the room and ripping his throat out with my bare hands and four plus years on I still do. How this man had never had the shit beaten out of him is beyond me but fuck I would have loved to have done it. These two people had, their entire lives, twisted and manipulated other human beings for their own personal gain just like Dr Haritha

Devineni did to me although purely for political gain. These people – Karen, Rex and the doctors from QLD health – were all chronic liars, I was completely appalled and disgusted.

I must also refer to the medical discharge report about the broken bone in my foot as suggested by Dr Renuka who also mentioned my belief that I had very good knowledge about the orthopaedics of the human body, a doctor's ego flaring yet again. The actual truth of the story I have already told you but I would strongly suggest that eight years of treatment and multiple surgeries was a little more than Dr Renuka's 'broken bone' in my foot; and yes, I studied seven days per week morning, day and night predominantly about the foot and ankle, after all it was my foot and I wanted to do as much as I could to help my surgeons as this was such a complex foot and ankle injury and trying to explain at times where all the pain was coming from was extremely difficult and tricky.

The Number One thing in my personal big picture was simply that I just wanted to walk again, nothing more and nothing less, just walk again. The report also suggested that I was working as a pastry chef for 30 hours per week, this was on the money but somewhat 50 hours short, I was working 80 hours per week in two different roles, excluding travel times and being paid overtime by neither, but still paid off AUD$2,000 on Rex Smith's credit card.

16 November 2017

This was one of the most shameful disgraces I had ever come across in my entire life. A so-called father putting his own son under immense pressure for money, so that he could keep living his champagne lifestyle on a home brewer's beer budget. This couldn't have been more the truth; I couldn't have tried harder to hit the truth right in the face. And the thing that gobsmacks me the most is everyone, including the Queensland government, swallowed everything that he had told them and completely denied all my protestations. I hoped karma would eventually catch up with them; this man and his deranged daughter could fool and brainwash just about anybody and everybody that questioned any part of their integrity, the funny thing was neither of them have any.

In 2016 karma did finally bite, and Rex Smith found himself with a major form of life-threatening illness, I guess it was fair to say that he was now living up to his primary reputation and the nickname of limp dick or as some prefer to call him, a soft cock. A chronic stress the size of the Melbourne cricket grounds had struck and for me it was about time, although far too slow – I would have wished for such a thing 20 years earlier, just to dampen that oversized ego and simply squash the cunt completely, but I was happy with this result, karma had finally been served.

Back to the report: the medications suggested within

had never been prescribed, except for Pristiq – known as Desvenlafaxine – and the bare minimum dose of a drug called Seroquel, known typically as Quetiapine. I was prescribed the minimum dose of 25 mg by my private psychiatrist Dr Jonathon Lichter purely to help me sleep and to try and improve my depressed mood, which was as a result of the anger and frustration brought on by the massive amounts of chronic and severe levels of pain which were crippling me. And I must say that not being not being able to walk was sending my anger and rage to a whole new level, this quite simply is something that words are never quite able to explain in full, but I am doing my best. Unless you have been in my shoes I would suggest that it's fair to say, "Shut your mouth and don't judge or comment until you have." But I must say on behalf of the infamous Dr Devineni and her team that an outrageous and staggering 32 times the dose of Seroquel (Quetiapine) was majorly excessive. These people, in my book, were absolute lunatics and to call themselves mental health doctors or as they preferred, psychiatrists, was nothing short of a disgrace. Oh and by the way, I never admitted to driving over speeds of 175 km/hr, simply because it never happened, this was just another one of their many fabricated lies and all the many words you read about 'child sex abuse, another family and a large sum of money and a house' were all entirely true. I had even offered to pay all of the caveat costs and offered to contribute towards the legal costs, but Rex Smith and my poor mum were just far too weak to take on a court battle that they would quite likely win once all the rock solid evidence had been put forward. They whinged about it to me and many other family members for years, but when it came to the crunch they both just turned their back on it, just as Rex did when he found out his three children had all been sexually abused by his father Frederick Stanley Smith, but I guess you couldn't expect anything less from a lifetime coward. In his mind he obviously thought it was okay to do nothing with the authorities about what had happened to his three children because at the end of the day I don't really think he cared, which I guess made him as bad as a paedophile itself, or quite possibly even worse, condoning the activities of a sexual predator is something I would never ever be able to understand, but I guess that's the difference between a real man and a coward. I had at least offered to kill my grandfather, and I wouldn't have had a problem with that, because quite honestly that is probably what should have happened. But no doubt I would have been jailed for a long and lengthy time over a complete piece of human scum and a downright low-life piece of shit, who others saw as a World War II hero, although let me tell you he was anything but a hero, and there were many very happy people to see and hear of his death, and I was top of that list.

And the car accident in the report with my daughter was quite simply that; a notorious piece of local road that had caught me by surprise, slipping on a massive film of micro sand, dust and tiny pieces of a gravel-like substance. The QLD police turned up and so did about 35–40 onlookers but the police did their job and that was it, no careless, reckless or erratic driving as suggested, just a simple single car accident. But, oh no, the two super heroes, the infamous Karen Justice and Rex Smith, had to take it further of course, these two dickheads just didn't know when to stop and had no idea how to mind their own business, they blew it to a whole new level, they are the two biggest drama queens I have ever known.

29 January 2018

Back to the so-called treating doctors and their team. I had never been so drugged in my entire life, which caused many health problems resulting in many post hospital complications for several years and months after my eventual release early in the new year of 2014.

After the horrendous 32 times the dose of Seroquel – recommended at a minimum dose of 25 mg, not the staggering dose of 800 mg which is the maximum dosage and literally sent me into a flat spin – the next drug that these lunatics prescribed to me on the Involuntary Treatment Order (ITO) was 20 mg of a potent and toxic drug known as Olanzapine.

When I presented this script to the then Terry White pharmacy at the Pacific Fair Shopping Centre on the Gold Coast the two senior pharmacists on duty were called and they asked who had prescribed this for me. I replied, "A consultant doctor by the name of Haritha Devineni working for Queensland mental health." They both quickly responded by telling me that they would not dispense this dosage of the drug, "Because this dose will quite likely kill you and between us we have never prescribed more than 10 mg of this particular drug daily." "Please," they both said, "Take our advice and don't pursue this prescription." I chuckled and said, "I have to as it is part of a strict court order requirement I am being kept under." But I heeded their advice and kept the script in safekeeping.

Finishing up now on the medical report and its many conflicting stories, allegations and the fabrications, I suggest – as does my forensic psychologist, Dr Tayne Garforth – that the straw that broke the camel's back was when my Christmas leave with the children was revoked and two male nurses dragged me into my room, stripped my shorts and underwear from my body and speared a three-quarter inch needle into my behind filled with Midazolam. Forcing a 42-year-old man to relive what had happened to him daily as a 6 ½ year-old was the most likely cause of my nervous breakdown. This for me personally was the biggest form of disgrace I had ever experienced in my adult life so far to date. I must say to those involved, including John the hotshot ex-military member, there is an open invitation for you – and up to 13 of your best male work colleagues – to have a chance to fight me in a boxing ring at your earliest convenience, and although I have a disability to my right leg I still encourage your participation as you may be quietly surprised at the outcome, or if it better suits your needs and requirements I could arrange for our event to be held in a locked cage environment just as you did to me. I seriously doubt that you will take me up on my once in a lifetime offer to you and your colleagues. I have gradually become aware that you would only drive down the one-way streets which are appropriate to you with the power and protection of the QLD government, so you're just another gutless coward trying to puff his chest with the full support of his power crazy colleagues. I would strongly suggest that the QLD mental health legislation have a major and very intricate investigation into providing a complete overhaul of its current system. And, as important, or more importantly, conduct thorough background checks on the imbeciles that are instigating these particular justice examination orders on friends and family members, because Karen 'no joy' Justice and the cowardly Rex Smith should have been charged and convicted years ago for their chronic mental and emotional abuse and, in certain cases of my own, physical abuse. After all, as a 6-year-old child I was caned on a weekly basis and sometimes regularly on a daily basis, but through research and study you will discover that this is the daily behaviour and mannerisms of a narcissistic sociopath. These two serial arseholes are both very, very sick and deranged human beings and, as my GP Dr Dennis McMahon has made me aware, people of this nature generally get away with blue murder pretty much their entire lives. Let me tell you, these two arseholes aren't getting away with a single thing if I have anything to do with it, this is one thing that's for sure.

5 February 2018

I guess after growing up in a tirade of domestic violence and constant abuse these different types of behaviour and mannerisms would undoubtedly affect those living under this ugly, messy and most of all trying and debilitating roof; many have suggested to me that if Rex Smith had been removed from the situation, penalised and locked up, things would have been much more peaceful and somewhat relaxed, but instead he had my mum institutionalised, when in actual fact he was the real problem; my mum was one of the best people any human being could ever meet.

One thing as a young child – and now as a grown 46-year-old man – I could never understand were the substantial and major personality changes in these two particular people Karen and Rex, in going from the public eye, where they were both deemed to be nothing other than saints while behind closed doors they were just out of control abusive lunatics to those closest to them. I always thought it was incredibly weird how people forgot things over time; let me tell you, I have forgotten absolutely nothing, I remembered all this traumatic abuse and violence, and just couldn't possibly delete one minute of it from my mind.

From the tender age of only five years old, the thing I remember most is Rex constantly verbally abusing my mum and then eventually me as well, never the two daughters. I remember vividly like yesterday that we were wrong in just about everything we said and most certainly everything we did in my entire life to date; something that still echoes in my mind is, 'Marj, you're wrong', 'Jeremy you're wrong', 'Marj you're wrong', 'Jeremy you're wrong', 'you're wrong', 'you're wrong'. These are classic traits of that of a super-controlling narcissistic sociopath, but only immediate family members and past husbands are totally aware of these two characters and the way they treated others, no doubt many work colleagues as well. Why my mum stayed with this abusive pig has always been beyond me, after all she rang me for many years to try and help get her out of the marriage and finally decided she was too old to be on her own and start afresh, but I most certainly would have looked after her, with no hesitation whatsoever. But as we all know fear is the reason why, pure and absolute fear on women's behalf. This is why he would never address the child sex abuse issues or the major physical and mental abuse I endured from my local employer as a very young 16-year-old apprentice. These people are all in the same category; they are all the biggest of cowards, the whole lot of them, they would only pick on the weak and incredibly vulnerable. One thing I have always lived by is to treat others the way I would like to be treated myself, because after all, I guess to many it is nice to be important but most of all, it is important to be nice.

Being a dad of three myself I had ensured that my children were treated with the utmost respect and I most certainly did not take out my personal troubles on them. I also guided them through life in the best way I know how, by not dictating to them what they could and couldn't do because after all they were themselves individuals. And I had made it incredibly clear that if someone messed with them in an inappropriate way, then they were messing with me as well, which quite simply wouldn't be the greatest of ideas. I was a dad who stuck by my children through thick and thin and that should be the duty of every parent because if they can't look to you for help and support, who do they look to? My solemn promise to my three children has remained firm and rock solid, my way of life through major unfortunate bouts of unnecessary sexual, physical and emotional abuse left me in such a way that I told my children as my lifelong promise to them that in the event of any form of abuse to ring me and I would be there in a flash, defuse the situation in my own way to ensure the safety of their personal wellbeing, and then call the police. The other way round – calling the police first – could and would likely cause loss of a life and as long as I was still breathing, I would do my utmost to ensure this never happened. After all from my personal experiences – and I make clear my personal experiences – it dawned on me how incredibly true it is that we've all heard people say constantly, 'you can choose your friends but you can't choose your family', that was one thing that was 100% for sure in life, just as death and taxes. And aren't they both just a shit of a thing, if we could avoid either or both, I'm sure most of us would.

Jeremy Smith

19 January 2018

Once we all lived in a great world but more importantly in what was once a great country, yes indeed, Australia. Sadly, this once great country is now riddled with political correctness and from where I stand Australia is in desperate need of a serious reality check, because I strongly suggest that we just need to go back to the good old-fashioned Yes or No, Right or Wrong, from my personal experience as well as that of several million Australians, this is when Australia was at its peak. However, all this bullshit does is stop human beings such as me from speaking to governing bodies and stopping people like myself from speaking the truth. We unfortunately are living in a coward's world, but most importantly we are living in a cowardly country. We honestly have a system and state and federal governments that support the cowards and the crooks, and which has tried to destroy true blue Aussies like me who say it how it is through circumstances that I explained earlier. But clearly – and more crystal clear than ever – there are some people who just don't like hearing the truth and you just can't argue with that, I know there are many hundreds of thousands in my boat that have been up against the same or similar battles, and much to my disgust the way people are treated in these public mental health facilities is simply an outrage, but as importantly, it's quite simply heartbreaking and soul destroying, and most of all it is completely inhumane. I have seen many media clips and several programs on animal cruelty that were nowhere near as bad as the treatment that was being dished out to human beings in these so-called public mental health facilities, there simply isn't anything the slightest bit healthy about them.

And I guess it is more than fair to say that doctors like Dr Haritha Devineni who diagnose people – including me – with the very serious mental illness of bipolar affective disorder, are being politically incorrect, but the many lawyers that I have consulted – including criminal and medical negligence lawyers – have strongly and firmly advised that this is not actually politically incorrect, it was, in fact, purely criminal, and so-called professionals pulling stunts like this to protect their own arses should be imprisoned and/or deported just as other everyday criminals are. But, as usual, working for the Queensland government – and in fact any government lately – these particular so-called professionals got away with blue murder on a daily basis, although I wasn't going to let Dr Haritha Devineni and her Indian team get away with this one. I was born a fighter but most of all I was born to be a survivor and all I wanted was acknowledgment, but more importantly I want justice. For an incredibly dedicated family man who has been through bankruptcy after a life-changing injury – and is still undergoing a current daily battle with chronic pain – and who just wanted to fill his children's Santa sacks with presents in the Christmas of 2013, but instead ended up being locked in an animal-like cage, is something that I don't really ever think I will manage to comprehend in full. And to enter such a Queensland health facility at a healthy body weight of 97 kg and be released some 21–22 days later at a staggering 115 kg with a chronic right leg injury is simply inexcusable. These low-life doctors had a lot to answer for and with a cost to me of one lost job and a dollar cost to my family of approximately AUD$27,000 it was quite simply nothing but a disgrace, and every day that I mentioned my loss of income to Dr Renuka and Dr Abby they just laughed in my face very arrogantly; they thrived on their warped sense of power, and this indeed has been acknowledged by Vicky Green and Dr Neeraj Gill in a meeting at the now new Gold Coast University Hospital in QLD. They both at least showed me significant common decency and a hell of a lot of respect unlike the aforementioned doctors. And I must mention that Dr Gill did remind me a lot of the medical genius Dr Aneel Nihal; professional, respectful, courteous and just a real good honest and down-to-earth decent human being and the same goes for Vicky Green, an acting director of Gold Coast hospitals. At least Dr Gill had the common decency and courtesy to apologise on behalf of the female Indian doctors, and I thank him for that, but one thing I was sure of was that I wouldn't like to be the senior consultant doctor in charge of those disrespectful bitches, and believe me I'm being extremely nice referring to them as bitches, to me they will always be human scum.

7 April 2018

On the basis of this whole situation and the mess in which the power crazy Campbell Newman's mental health legislation found me, together with a completely deranged extended family who were trying to cover up the fact that all three children had been chronically sexually abused by Rex Stanley Smith's father, Frederick Stanley Smith, I find it utterly appalling that people just wouldn't and couldn't accept the truth, because of excessive forms of personality weaknesses and most importantly the highest level of cowardice. But I must make mention that no less than 75% of the mental health services staff constantly said to my face, mainly in twos or threes, "We just can't understand for the life of us why and how you are in this facility." I replied, "When you have a completely deranged sister and two parents that are desperately trying to cover up the truth, this is most definitely how I have ended up in here." Most agreed that my sister should have been indefinitely institutionalised, but when people fabricate lies and manipulate the actual truth, the innocent always end up being crucified; I most certainly was.

However, I do have to mention if people like Aidah, Bettina, Alberto and most importantly the lovely Filipino Agnes hadn't been there, I would have stayed in the institution for many more weeks than I did. These particular four human beings I will never ever forget, they were all very compassionate, loving and caring, but most of all they were honest. They are sensational human beings, and I sincerely thank them for everything.

26 April 2018

As time went on and all the very sincere and genuine people, including my uncle Bill Mackinley, continued to tell me that time did, in fact, heal almost anything and everything which, as an adult I had always believed anyway, I discovered that it did. Except for my disabled right foot and ankle, that chronic and debilitating pain which failed to go away and played a huge part of making me feel worthless on a daily basis. But I must report that at a staggering four years post my cage experience I began to sleep in a more restored and normal way. After my personal ordeal with these Queensland government dickheads, it was hard to believe with such out of control levels of stress and anxiety that I would actually ever sleep properly again, however, with such a massive psychiatric agitation I was just doing the best I knew how to under the circumstances, and yes, without any of those potent and deadly prescription medications.

3 June 2018

At some time in late March/early April 2018 I was couch bound as usual watching Channel Nine's "Ellen" show – yes, believe it or not a bloke watching "Ellen" – and she said something to a guest on her program about the struggles she had endured in her life and how she had managed to overcome several of them and it was then, at my age of 46 years young, that she triggered something in my mind to approach a very new and fresh angle to tackle the disability of this mongrel right foot and ankle of mine. Even with excessive levels of debilitating and chronic pain and sheer mental exhaustion from trying to use the limb, as well as lack of sleep due to pain levels 24/7, thanks to "Ellen" I picked up the phone and started calling doctors, surgeons and a few Brisbane-based hospitals trying to track down a man by the name of Dr Ben Forster. He was another renowned foot and ankle surgeon who, by just talking to other patients, some random general practitioners and people in basic public places such as supermarkets, petrol stations, coffee shops, etc. I discovered had a great reputation. After much research and many, many phone calls, and about 6–8 months I eventually tracked him down and thanks to a telephone arranged referral from my GP of 27 years Dr Dennis McMahon from the Gold Coast, Queensland, arranged to meet with him, initially with my daughter Georgia on the 4th May 2018.

Dr McMahon is seriously a genuine true blue top Aussie bloke, he is in the Top 5 men I have ever met in my life; he helped me and steered me through my mess, heartache and more importantly, my complete nervous breakdown thanks to QLD mental health, Karen Justice and Rex Smith. He was disgusted and appalled by the treatment I'd had to endure and especially the way in which my so-called extended family had dealt with and handled things. But he always tried to reassure me and instil faith that I would make a full recovery and feel better mentally over time, and he was absolutely spot on.

I had decided on this particular "Ellen" day that I was just far too young to give up and throw in the towel, but shit I had come incredibly close, that was for sure, purely just because of my difficultly and the exhaustion of getting from point A to point B. Somehow I just kept managing to dig deeper than I had ever had to dig, and remarkably, I found the smallest amount of the highest personal octane fuel to restart the entire process all over again, after that last surgery in November 2016 where Dr Hope and I had decided to hang up the scalpel, remembering that each surgery has a minimum 9–12 months' recovery time.

After an incredibly long and very slow year of 2017, I was most certainly beginning to restore and find my personal inner strength; I was very, very slowly but definitely regathering the personal emotional and psychological strength equivalent to that of a very poorly tuned 350 Chev, but I was certainly on the way back up. Although I was always shit scared of falling and collapsing in a written-off pile of mess again, as long as I kept Karen 'no joy' Justice, Rex Smith and Haritha Devineni out of my life, the possibility of me allowing this to happen again was slim.

I have always referred to and compared human beings, especially myself, to cars. One thing for sure was though that a very high percentage of cars can be repaired, but from personal experience, the human body can't. Especially when you have had major damage to a crucial part of your chassis – which indeed I did – I had made an incredibly tough and firm decision to keep fighting, it was in my blood, just as the love of fast cars and motorbikes is. I suppose with a very overly judgemental extended family and high levels of abuse and neglect, I had two choices in life and that was to keep fighting or lie down and die; my choice was to keep fighting. And I most certainly couldn't ignore my actual inner and gut feelings and what my brain was telling me to do, and that simply was, 'mate, just keep going, you have proven to yourself that you still have enough inner mongrel to keep battling on,' so quite honestly quitting wasn't an option, but fuck me, even though I was so incredibly spent, my 'me' just wouldn't allow it, so fight on I did. I had to personally and seriously work on that poorly tuned 350 Chev and turn it back into a port and polished blue printed honed 355 stroker[19], but shit it was awkwardly tricky.

7 June 2018

Approaching 10 years with this injury it's more than fair to say that my last 9.7 years are a blur. And even though such a significant amount of time has passed I have to admit I still struggle daily to try and comprehend how the Flying Fox could have had such a defining change in which the ways and different forms of my life had changed. I know there are many hundreds of thousands of human beings who have had illnesses and injuries way worse than mine, but everything is relevant to the individual and I can say that because of this personal confusion, relayed to me by that pain 24 hours per day, seven days per week. That was the primary reason for

---

19. Engine terminology, cylinder port where the piston fires.

the incomprehension, I was reminded by it every minute of every day and that was incredibly tough, not to mention the sheer hellish nightmare Karen, Rex and QLD Health managed to force upon me; it seriously had been a very cloudy 10 years. And now only yesterday on the 6th June 2018 I was informed that a sincerely great friend and neighbour "Poppy John" had passed away; he was a real, true blue, fair, dinkum Aussie man who had helped me massively with my personal mess. He and I had many discussions about life and I seriously looked up to him as a father figure role model, something that I had never really had, just abuse after abuse and negative after negative. Quite honestly getting away from my biological father was probably the best thing I had ever done, I know for sure "Poppy John's" two sons didn't want to get away from him, he respected and supported them, and I was sincerely gutted when his wife notified me of his passing, because the world needs more men like him.

Getting back to Dr Ben Forster, his surgical proposal to me was to remove both peroneal tendons in my right foot and ankle, completely sever my peroneal longus and remove both, and remove the most obliterated part of my peroneal brevis tendon and replace it with the best sample of my right hamstring tendon he could find. I must say that it was weird and unbelievably scary to replace two major tendons that connected the leg to the foot with only one tendon piece selected from the back of my upper leg. It was hard to listen to him tell me that he was going to discard two of the most crucial tendons in the human body, and when he told me that globally the minimum number of people to have this particular procedure was 1%, that was a no-brainer, but when he hit me with the maximum figure of only 2% an instantaneous wave of emotion rippled through my entire body and the moment I left his office and the actual hospital itself, the dam wall broke, and as I tried and tried desperately to turn off my personal burst water pipe I continuously failed in doing so. More shell shocking news; I just wasn't sure how much more bad news I could keep receiving, but really I had no choice, these were the cards I had been dealt and there was no escaping it, this was reality and this, indeed, was part of life. But what was going through my mind in a supercharged form of lightning bolt speed only I could try to understand.

Those racing thoughts were incredibly distressing to me, but the two things that stood out the most like balls on a bull were, if only those serial arseholes in Byron Bay – yes Karen 'no joy' Justice and the super hero himself Rex Smith – had the slightest idea of how much personal grief this had caused me, perhaps they wouldn't have tried to be the fuckwit superheros that they both thought they were. I know, and only I know, that these two idiots simply just didn't have a clue or the personal inner strength to last more than 18 months past my original accident and injury date, because they are both seriously and utterly incredibly piss weak human beings, and this is, in fact, a major part of their pernicious nature. The other main thing that kept flashing in and out of my mind faster than the speed of light was that, shit I was 37 when my nightmare began to unfold and next month I turn 47, how in the hell did this all happen and where did that ten years of my life go? I guess to me the most important thing is that my three children still manage to have a beautiful smile on each and every one of their faces, and to me with what they have all been through as well, that quite simply is not only remarkable but, in fact, a sensational bonus and they are what keep me going; it is the combination of my extreme love for my children, my passion for cars, motorbikes and music for which I am incredibly grateful. As a dad I am so blessed to have such beautiful children, most importantly happy and healthy children, but what they have all been through was totally and completely unnecessary, they all now have unwanted baggage as well.

25 June 2018

One thing through all this I have felt become stronger and stronger as this journey and my injury – together with my story as it unfolded – is my supercharged passion. And my ultimate desire to race around the global phenomenon and iconic landmark of Mount Panorama Circuit in Bathurst, NSW, Australia in any high-powered V8 car became so intense within my heart and soul that this is what encouraged me to fight on, because with such a life-changing injury that had majorly affected my accelerator foot, words just can't quite explain how seriously important it was for me on a personal basis to conquer, purely just to prove a point to myself, and my personal best mates and my three beautiful children were all my biggest support in this. And when I urged my surgeon Dr Matthew Hope several times of the importance of this being made possible to happen much to his disbelief, he assured me 100% that my right foot was more than capable of being able to achieve such a lifelong goal. His words were, as he rolled his eyes, "Yes, your foot is completely capable of braking at 300 km/hr," and for me if this was the prize for all of this incredible personal heartache it was truly worth fighting for because, quite simply, in my life that was all that really mattered and if I could conquer and complete my ultimate lifelong dream since those early days of being with Uncle Bruce I could honestly say my mission was complete.

As I wrote previously I admit that my serious head over heels love and passion for fast cars and motorbikes and my favourite collection of music is, in actual fact, together with my serious love for my children, how I managed to pull myself from the deepest, dark black hole of depression; as tough as it was with so many different negatives in my life, including my own extended family with their complete and utterly deranged way of thinking and their major lack of empathy my dream quite simply is what has kept me alive. I would be interested to see how long they all would have lasted mentally not being able to walk more than 35–50 metres unaided and then collapsing in a buckled heap of incomprehensible pain and a tsunami of tears; I reckon not more than 6–12 months maximum, and I am incredibly proud that I have lasted almost 10 years.

My incredibly serious approach to focus only on all my passionate and seriously intense positives in my life is how I have pulled it off and, if the many circus clowns who have judged me thus far had in their life been through exactly what I have in mine – they simply have absolutely no idea, but if they had – I'd like to hear that their journey wasn't without the heartache I suffered, because if they said it was completely trouble free they would simply be speaking rubbish and a whole heap of bullshit. All of the idiots who believed they understood what I had been through over time have actually no idea and clearly lack intelligence, empathy and most importantly have no real idea about life itself and the many very complicated challenges that can arise, full stop.

Jeremy Smith

For me personally the fact that so many lives have been tragically lost through unbeaten levels of depression is simply heartbreaking, especially for the many families that have suffered the loss of loved ones; this is something that absolutely nobody deserves, and it has often brought many a tear to my eye. I must say that public health systems making such pecuniary decisions through these power crazy psychiatrists and their mental health departments and tribunals I, and many hundreds of fellow Queenslanders, just don't deserve such psychiatric agitation or false and misleading diagnosis such as the serious mental illness of bipolar affective disorder; these people deserve to be put behind bars, and to be real honest and frank from where I am standing that is exactly what needs to happen and I just can't see it from any other angle other than that, me and many hundreds of people with whom I share my story. Their ways and their treatment, and indeed their conduct, was just beyond inhumane and completely against all forms of human rights legislation and these particular arseholes at Robina Hospital in Queensland, together with their overly inflated egos and their mannerisms were what would tip a lot of people over the edge; I had been very close, but am incredibly grateful that I actually lived to tell my story and I am extremely proud of that too.

4 August 2018

I am the type of human being who is strongly against these particular forms of treatment that are nothing more than chronic levels of psychological and physical abuse. What I indeed experienced together with what I saw happen to others I wouldn't wish upon anyone, but I'd be lying if I didn't admit that I would like to see Haritha Devineni, Karen 'no joy' Justice and Rex Stanley Smith get put through their paces, but with me in charge this time because not one of those spineless lowlifes would be able to sustain the really high levels of mental and emotional abuse. These particular three human beings were actually born not only to abuse, but most definitely neglect people; none of them have a loving or compassionate bone within their bodies, all of them thrive purely on copious and constant power, and to me, through so many personal experiences with these people they are all just the lowest low-life levels of hunks of shit the world could possibly produce, all chasing the same delusional sense of the exact same thing, power.

I have always sincerely loved even in desperate situations through my own life of constant and chronic bullying, abuse and equally, neglect. My heart is easily and quickly broken when I see people being knocked down mentally and emotionally and, a lot of the time, physically; I have always found it personally impossible not to intervene and though these chronic and constant levels of abuse and neglect have hardened me into a human being that I can honestly say I wish I could change, there have been many times in public where I have peeled low-life thugs off the so many soft, weak and incredibly vulnerable, something I once was. I simply could never have kept count of that, however, the many taps on the back I have received from mostly ladies seeking help was certainly countless over the years. And as many of these ladies have said to me, "the world needs more men like you and if we ever have to go to war, I want to be in the trenches with you, because undoubtedly we will be safe with you." Unabashedly, I agreed, I would never go around beating people up in general public, but I was never afraid of putting them in their place if they were assaulting somebody else; to me it is seriously heartbreaking and soul destroying for everyone involved, except the actual bully themselves, somehow in some weird and wonderful way it makes them feel good and that is something I will never understand, not even in two lifetimes. Once I had disengaged them from their victim I always offered abusive pigs – who thrived on beating and assaulting the weak and vulnerable – ten of their best and greatest shots at me before I would lay one finger on them, and to date in all these many public situations not one person ever took me up on my more than generous offer, which always made me chuckle; they only picked on those weaker than themselves and weren't prepared to have a crack at a more evenly matched opponent. Because, after all, in arguing and fighting there were never ever really any winners unless, I guess, you were boxing for some kind of world title, all it did was cause significant heartbreak one way or another, generally to everyone involved. But I will always stick up for the soft, weak and incredibly vulnerable as long as I am still breathing; I detest and despise bullying every which way, but sadly it was part of growing up and more importantly it was indeed part of my life. I could, in fact, fight like Tyson, but I chose not to, and anyone that thinks bullying is ever going to go away ever, seriously needs their head read. It's up to blokes like myself to try and stop all forms of abuse by simply trying to calm people, sit down and have a serious heart-to-heart chat with them and offer the best form of support you possibly can, but sadly this never really happens due to human beings' selfishness; I certainly wasn't and never have been in that category, I was always only about putting smiles back on people's faces in the best and quickest way possible I knew how.

The thing that made me laugh out loud and sometimes even uncontrollably was that both Karen 'no joy' Justice and Rex Stanley Smith thrived on dishing it out with their vicious, and most of the time, uncontrollable mouths and their overly abusive personal savage and attacking personalities; they simply couldn't take one word of anything back and I must say their major levels of personal weaknesses made me feel satisfied in that it proved that they were true narcissists; Haritha Devineni is also in this category, only she was hiding behind a Queensland government badge and there is no denying that.

I have spoken to many different paramedic teams in public, and when they eventually ask about my crook leg[20] and what caused it, I tell them of the sheer hell it has caused me and what I have been put through by QLD health and they all shake their heads in disgust and disbelief, but also admit that this happens on a day to day basis and that they are ashamed by what these so-called doctors get away with on a daily, weekly, and annual basis; they agree it was overuse and abuse of Queensland government power and I find this even more disturbing, but those ambulance officers and everyone else who I have confided in are all of the same opinion that I was indeed a person who says it how it is and nobody, including my extended family or even those grubby doctors, could stand to listen to the ultimate truth, and that was spot on. I can sincerely and honestly say this it was no fun being locked in cages under a court order and forced to

---

20. Australian slang for bad, not working, etc. or if someone is unwell.

take toxic levels of medication, not only against my own free will, but that I actually didn't need.

In my entire life of holding a driver's licence I have never driven past a lady at the roadside with a flat tyre as I am very aware that most have absolutely no chance of cracking those wheel nuts, let alone jacking up the vehicle and being able to lift not one but two wheels, but the way in which Dr Haritha Devineni, Dr Ranuka and Dr Abby have represented the female population, together with all their many fabricated false and misleading allegations and chronic perjury in the lies they had written about me, has turned me against women in general. I now sadly keep driving right past the female stranded on the roadside with that puncture, always with Karen, Haritha, Ranuka and Abby heavily stamped into the back of my mind. I have even had letters written to past employers from ladies in trouble at the roadside thanking me for my sincere help and most of all, my generosity. The only female I now look after and show love and respect to is my daughter.

Through my years of research about psychiatrists who are considered to be at the top of the medical hierarchy food chain I found out quite a few things that are not only astonishing, but seriously disturbing in the way their power crazy deranged minds actually function; they truly and honestly believe they are above the law – although not all of them; it is fair to say the good old 80–20 principle applies here too.

1. Doctor Donald Grant, a former QLD government forensic psychiatrist consultant who betrayed a QLD-based mother by publishing a book in which the content spoke about her daughter's death, and yet she was completely unaware of how her murder had been committed, thanks to QLD government regulations.
2. Doctor Haritha Devineni, current QLD government consultant psychiatrist diagnosing patients with serious mental illnesses purely to prevent any possibility of any form of litigation, including from me.
3. Doctor Stephen Frieberg of Sydney, NSW, diagnosing a very close personal friend of mine – purely trying to defend himself through breaches of an EBA[21] and multiple accounts of unfavourable treatment by a local QLD corporate giant employer – with severe chronic paranoid personality disorder (PPD) which consists of narcissistic, histrionic and antisocial traits and can also indicate murderous rage.
4. Doctor Jean Eric Gassy, an Adelaide-based Indian

---

21. Enterprise bargaining agreement.

psychiatrist who was deregistered as a medical practitioner, now incarcerated in a Yatala based prison in south Australia with a conviction of murder and sentenced to a 30-year imprisonment without parole.

5. Doctor Margaret Tobin, former head of mental health services, south Australia. This particular mental health professional was murdered by one of her former employees, the above-mentioned deregistered Indian born Jean Eric Gassy. Doctor Tobin was shot four times in the head in a South Australian hospital on the 14th October 2002.

After my brief research it was evident and crystal clear to me that these psychiatrists were beyond deranged and delusional and obviously capable of pretty much anything and everything as their obsession with power was through the roof, so yes, capable of anything, including the brutal crime of murder. These particular people were not only a significant danger to themselves, but more importantly they were an extreme and major danger to the general public and society as a whole.

I strongly suggest that if Doctor Haritha Devineni continues to treat people as she did me, it is most certainly imminent that she will end up with the same fate as Dr Tobin; it's not a matter of what or if but when her overly abusive obsession of power and her incredibly pernicious attitude will, I truly and honestly believe, eventually catch up with her. In my book she can have her power crazy QLD government employee role because I most certainly wouldn't want to be ill-treating general members of public as she does, because if I did, I know I would never sleep at night, understanding clearly how she abuses people, but then she readily has access to many toxic pharmaceutical drugs that I guess, in turn, would help her with a favourable night's sleep.

The way in which the entire male population, and especially adult men, is treated within Australia's many failing systems makes it ridiculously clear to me and many of my friends, both female and male, that these governments have simply lost their way and should give men back some kind of rights; they have to allow men to defend themselves because in so many cases – actually 65% plus according to police statistics – it is, in fact, female provocation with words and actions that have caused a vast majority of heartache including my situation but, as we all know, they can say and do pretty much whatever they want and this quite simply is wrong. It's a no-brainer to me that giving the male population back a small window of defence opportunity would keep so many women alive which is a great thing, but the current system which is hellbent on crushing men in the best possible way is wholly and solely wrong. And, as importantly, we need to stop the daily growing number of men within Australia committing suicide with male suicide currently at an all-time national high; these statistics speak for themselves, most definitely something within the system is failing severely. For me and so many millions of the Australian public – both men and women – all this domestic violence and its consequences, leaving children without a mummy or a daddy is not only completely soul destroying but devastatingly heartbreaking, these courts have some serious answering to do.

The growing number of female power crazy politicians need a significantly short and long-term reality check of the big picture, because with their obsession with power and destroying men they just don't realise that they are, in fact, the cause of this everyday domestic violence; their delusional obsession of power has allowed this serious problem to get out of control. I, along with many millions of fellow Australians, am not really impressed with how they're dealing with these many different situations including men; I often wonder how they would feel if the tides were reversed, how would they like to have absolutely no rights, I suggest that they wouldn't enjoy it one little bit, when indeed, so many of them have deeply abused all of their many women's rights, which is an utter disgrace.

Jeremy Smith

With collusion and corruption within the state government and even more rife and riddled throughout the entire federal government as well as in the many local and community based authorities, and indeed the actual courts themselves, it is clearer than the noses on all our faces that Australia has 100% completely lost its way in so many different aspects and faculties in which how our once great country was being managed. For Christ's sake will the people with the so-called "power" start capturing and prosecuting the right people – yes, including many women, not just men – and hand them down the correct, appropriate and warranting penalties, because our entire justice system is getting it wrong pretty much most of the time; daily, weekly and yearly including the unnecessary fucking bullshit that I was forced to endure, purely for wanting to pursue and try my hand at, something I had dreamed of since I was a four or five year old little boy – yes, my absolute ultimate passion, racing cars. I still struggle to comprehend this entire mess some five years on and probably will for the rest of my life. But I guess the answer to my many questions and the so many different variables all come back to the same disturbing common denominator, that is, the deranged and very unconventional mind of the delusional Karen 'no joy' Justice, someone who truly believes she is somewhere between Queen Elizabeth, Julia Gillard and Wonder Woman. But it is undeniably true that the horseshit

I was forced to take part in only happened simply because I don't have a vagina and/or a set of chest-pushing breasts, but I do have a penis and if I didn't explain it in this particular 'hit the nail on the head' way, then I would have to admit that I too am telling porky pies just like the so many false and misleading allegations that have been written about me; in fact, thanks to the very hard-working and legitimate everyday Australian taxpayers, these power crazy dickhead government people receive a more than generous salary package to lie professionally on a day to day basis. It is seriously sad but true, not just for me but for so many of my mates and even more for so many millions of fellow Australians, that the map of Tasmania is in fact trying to take over and dictate to the entire big map and even bigger picture of Australia.

8 October 2018

I guess after digesting everything comprehensively in full since my horrifying experience back on the 15th December 2013, one of the most disturbing things I have ever been exposed to and involved in was when not one but, in fact, five or six Queensland government psychiatrists employed by the Robina Hospital Queensland pretty much dragged me into the boardroom for patients and doctors without any of my allied persons – which is pretty much illegal according to my personal research – and sat me down like a three-year-old in a day care centre, only there was no care, and simply and quickly said, "Jeremy, you are bipolar, you are bipolar, you are bipolar, you are bipolar, you are bipolar." I just laughed and laughed at all of them and said, "you are entirely and completely fucked in the head," and continued to say that I truly believed that they didn't have the slightest clue what they were doing, I hadn't even spoken to any of these other circus clowns except for Wonder Woman herself, Haritha Devineni, and Ranuka and Abby. This was collusion at its ultimate and incredibly corrupt level like I had never seen before, but in time I will deal with every single one of these idiots in a supreme court or preferably the federal court one by one; I am not taking this bullshit from anybody, I don't give a flying fuck who they are, I had done nothing wrong. I respect no one who simply doesn't show any sign of respect towards me, and to be honest I've had a complete gutful and am fed up with the dishonesty from massive, savage and chronic collusion and corruption, and to be quite frank I am up to the eyeballs with it, enough is enough, this bullshit has to stop. These Queensland government psychiatric dickheads need serious reprimanding and should be penalised in a court of law, they are all soft, incredibly weak and equally pathetic but most of all incredibly dishonest, just as were Karen 'no joy' Justice and Rex 'no balls' Stanley Smith. You must remember all of you current and ex-government employees who don't know your arse from your elbow, remember I had a perfect record every which way! Oh, but these psychiatric doctors truly did believe they were the elite, but let me tell you that they couldn't be further from the truth, they are all incredibly and unbelievably deranged; warped with delusional minds and a sense of the significant greatness of power, because after all every single human being is capable of having a target on their head, and these characters are primed for that over time if they continue to treat people the way they treated me.

One always wonders why these fruit loop so-called mental health professionals or believe-it-or-not doctors treat their family members like worthless pieces of shit like my family did me with their over-ambitious levels and obsession with power. Do they always believe they are right about everything and anything just as Karen 'no joy' Justice and Rex 'no balls' Stanley Smith do? My guess is that they probably do. I stand firmly that they do because after all they are the elite in the medical world, and they actually believe all of their own bullshit, and that they actually do know what is going on in someone else's head. What a wayward incredible load of bullshit; the only thing that they did do well, in my experience, was lie to the best of their ability. The other thing that they did really well was exceed at accomplishing a very dishonest day's work funded by the extremely hard-working Australian taxpayer; they had individual competitions with one another to see who could fill out an entire prescription pad the quickest, who would actually receive the gold, silver and the bronze. I would sincerely suggest that that was the ultimate challenge for each one of them, week in and week out, and no doubt laugh about it, like they did to my face every time I questioned their judgement. But it would be fair to say that no doubt the Indian angel trio who laughed in people's faces including mine and enjoyed humiliating people at the highest possible level they knew how, are probably not laughing too much now, the low-life pieces of human scum.

28 October 2018

In wishing to advise the parents of today realising how much worse and severely savage the world has become in every which way, I would strongly suggest that the many tens of thousands of new age parents should watch their children very, very closely, but more importantly at the top of their list, definitely listen to their children very carefully and intricately and what they have to say using their own words of defence and judgement. Please whatever you do, don't be like my mother and say constantly, "Come on, stop being silly." Let me make you deeply aware that being sexually abused almost daily for a period of close to two years, that there was nothing silly about it. Believe me when I say the fear is simply indescribable, I just was never able to put it into words, but what I did know was that for the two years I suffered sexual abuse from my grandfather the sky-high level of fear caused me to wet my bed between 2–5 times per night and that is something that no child should ever, ever, have to endure.

In one of my very many sessions my personal counsellor, Dr Tayne Garforth, who holds a PhD in psychology and in forensic psychology suggested to me on the 7th November 2016 that indeed, I was simply a product of horrendous parental neglect and equally of severe abuse which caused me to have extremely high levels of anxiety, which I agree with undoubtedly. I must say that with the so many hundreds and hundreds of questions that I had asked myself over so many years it was somewhat of a significant relief to hear it come from a very real mental health professional. To date she is by far the smartest female I have ever met by a country mile in my lifetime, she seriously is true blue. She is completely unlike the delusional fruit loop psychiatric team led by Dr Haritha Devineni at the Robina hospital on the Gold Coast of Queensland. Please parents of today, please support your children in every which way that you possibly can, not just one out of three like my parents did, support and love your children equally through both the easy and, more importantly, the extremely hard times even more, because after all, children in their younger years especially need a hell of a lot more than just three meals a day, a bed, several sets of clothes and a bath or shower and a toothbrush; they need loads of love, care and nurturing, but most of all they need to know and understand that in times of severe and desperate need, regardless of the trauma or incident, that you will always be there for them and care for them in every which way, regardless of the extremity of the crime which may have been committed against them, because in my case there were so many times but I had to learn how to deal with the situation the best way I knew how from age 6 ½ years, so this is where my parents failed at the highest possible level.

Please, whatever you do, don't be weak and pathetic like my parents were and end up living half a lifetime in denial, always trying to tell themselves that the way they handled things with their three sexually abused children was okay; believe me when I say it most certainly wasn't, they couldn't have been more wrong if they had tried, turning their back on their own children was something that they would both have to take with them to their graves.

As a parent and dad of three children myself, one thing for sure was that I monitored every single one of my three children very closely and if there were any problems with any of them I would deal with and fix the problem immediately, small or large, knowing full well that if I didn't the problem would manifest over time and become bigger than Texas just as it was with my own personal messy situation. I'm so extremely grateful that I never lacked personal strength of character and certainly showed no signs of weakness in my personality and no doubt so are my three children.

With society – and most certainly new age adult humans – slowly but surely becoming more gutsy and clearly and obviously becoming more outspoken and finding the emotional and psychological strength to start standing up for themselves, most definitely gives me a personal sense of calm, by virtue of the fact that people are actually beginning to want to defend themselves against these sickening and outrageously despicable and seriously criminal figures such as paedophiles, rapists and murderers, and what directly gives me even more emotional and psychological calm is simply that so many hundreds of thousands of serial carpet sweepers from the 1930s and the 1940s are slowly but surely being phased out through their passing and thank god for that. Covering up crime, especially against young and innocent incredibly vulnerable children, most definitely and simply is not only completely unforgivable but, much more importantly, it is most certainly equally unforgettable; my horrifying memories are seared firmly in the back of my mind for the rest of my life.

30 October 2018

If only I could have walked into the local police station at the tender age of 6–7 years old I more than likely would have been there almost daily, reporting the physical and mental abuse from both Rex Stanley Smith and Karen Joy Smith and even more horrifying, the sexual abuse and criminal conduct of the World War II hero, the gut-wrenching and sickening paedophile, Frederick Stanley Smith. Both Rex and Karen Smith were both guilty of significant amounts of abuse against a minor and equally substantial amounts of neglect as well. No wonder that weak pathetic coward Rex Stanley Smith wouldn't speak up and protect me from the violent behaviour of both Greg and Wayne Earea because he was exactly the same, not quite as savage, but not far off, and I speak for myself and even more for my mother, but she was far too soft and weak to stand up to such an abusive pig, Rex Smith. But as far as not being able to walk into that police station of Byron Bay 2481 from around the age of six, I didn't actually start to understand the enormity of the abuse against an innocent child/teenager until about age 35; I was just far too young to even begin to try and comprehend, all

I knew was that something was really wrong, and I had to learn extremely early in life the meaning of survival and how to stay alive in the best way possible.

For the life of me I will never understand why Rex Stanley Smith made it into the local base Lismore published and printed paper, The Northern Star on Saturday 12 July 2014, looking for public sympathy over not knowing who his biological father was. Personally, all I could put it down to was not only his obsession with power but, more importantly, his absolute need for public attention – classic traits of a narcissist, but honestly who really cares, I certainly don't. This simply for me and my family and my very close personal mates was purely just another stage of his denial process which undoubtedly caused a psychological distraction within as well as trying to fool the local people that he had been hard done by. What he failed to tell the general public in his local region was that I had just got off an almost five-month QLD court order that had been instigated by the deranged Karen 'no joy' Justice and executed by the infamous money expert Rex Stanley Smith. Something I would never, ever understand in full was that the two people who needed to be institutionalised and imprisoned were undoubtedly and most definitely Karen Joy Justice and Rex Stanley Smith for their vicious and savage approach to others when things weren't going their way. Once they had ganged up on you, you were simply fucked, but you only have to ask several ex-husbands and my mother and indeed, if they were to tell you the truth, they would tell you they were both far from perfect role models as human beings, and if you did anything better than them in terms of achievement, look out because they just couldn't stand it. They both suffered from chronic 'tall poppy syndrome'[22], I guess that was because just about everything they touched business wise and financially they both failed at significantly; to me in our extended family they were the only two who were allowed to achieve, but the fact of the matter was that both of them were pretty much useless at anything and everything they touched and were ever involved in.

 I just laughed and laughed and laughed as I had hundreds of awards from my many personal achievements, but apparently you weren't allowed to acknowledge or admire the content and merit of your own personal achievements and you certainly would make no mention of your many awards as this definitely would be classed as grandiosity and part of a manic phase but, more importantly, this was categorised together with the love and passion for fast cars

---

22. The tall poppy syndrome describes aspects of a culture where people of high status are resented, attacked, cut down, strung up or criticised because they have been classified as superior to their peers. Wikipedia. https://en.wikipedia.org/wiki/Tall_poppy_syndrome [Accessed: 12 May 2019].

and motorbikes into a psychiatric illness better known as bipolar affective disorder... what a fucking load of bullshit.

My many great mates who have achieved through high levels of self-confidence must believe that they too must be suffering from the mental illness of bipolar affective disorder.

I can honestly say that after just over 30 years I can still see Karen with that cast iron fire stoke in front of the fireplace at the once named Everglades at only 6 ½ years of age and I can still feel that cane from Rex hitting my lower back and my bottom and his hand lifting me off the carpet that he chose to sweep things under as he struck me with extreme adult force. But what is embedded the most in the deepest part of my brain on a daily basis is when I am busting for a wee I still see and feel those knives brushing past the side of my ears and my face, and I must say the sound of those three-strap bread tins smashing into the stainless steel bench where I stood to work is a sound that will haunt me for the rest of my life, just as the urine dribbling down the inside of legs and into my shoes and socks is something my brain just won't allow me to forget; this extreme level of violence and its horrifying memories are with me forever.

One thing though that I am extremely happy and proud to share is that after a staggering 39 years now at age 47 when I drop the soap in the shower, I no longer see Frederick

Jeremy Smith

Stanley Smith's ugly, sickening and disgusting feet as I bend slowly to retrieve that cake of soap, but unfortunately his dirty old man body odour smell still remains to linger on and off as I turn on the hot water and it begins to steam. Words just can't explain how overjoyed I am that these events and their memories are slowly but surely beginning to ease, and I am extremely proud to be experiencing that. But all this is just extreme, severe and long-lasting psychological scarring that very slowly and most surely, I hope, will eventually completely fade away just as Byron Bay did in the rear-view mirror of my car some 26 years ago back in October 1992. Getting to the Ewingsdale turn-off for the final time, and turning right to venture north for a new beginning is probably the best decision I have made in my life to date, but if I am completely honest I would have preferred to stay in Greystanes Sydney, NSW, I would have preferred to stay in the care of Aunty Betty and Uncle Bruce, Phillip, Peter and Paul Townsend because they were the greatest family that I had ever met as a little boy, but at 6 ½ years this actually wasn't to be. I honestly believe it's fair to say that I wish I could have pressed those ALT, CTRL and DELETE buttons all at once as we can on modern-day computers, to delete and permanently remove those savage memories from my mind, but I know this is impossible, I guess I just have to learn to live with it and I have.

But the best thing to come from all of this I guess is that I learned at an extreme ultimate level how not to treat people and this is for sure, make no mistake I certainly am not afraid to tell the truth. I am not one little bit scared anymore to send any of these arseholes in Byron Bay and/or from the Robina to jail, because honestly that's where these low-life parasites and cowards deserve to be and many people agree with me, including my own personal professionals with whom I have consulted in many various ways.

I am also extremely proud to share and announce that I have handled and dealt with all these majorly traumatic levels of heartache and significantly high levels of personal stress without any form of substance abuse or alcoholism, although I have to admit I honestly would never have been able to manage or deal with any of these frightening and trying traumas without the help and psychological numbness that gambling provided. I must say though, that I have met some of the greatest people from many different parts of the world in the numerous different gambling venues I had visited over so many years and shared many a story, and while I can't say that I'm proud of being a lifelong gambler, I am proud to admit that I wouldn't be alive today without it, as it was my drug of choice – oh, and by the way, I don't ingest any form of antidepressant drugs or any of those wicked antipsychotics that were barrelled into me by the kilo at the Robina Hospital. I've just learned how to deal with it the best possible way I know how and many, many sincere thanks to Jonathon Lichter, the doctor who Haritha Devineni and her team chose to use as their scapegoat, and especially to the beautiful and amazing Dr Tayne Garforth. I did take some pain medication to help me get to sleep, and I must admit I wasn't keen on that either, I just was never really keen on the consumption of tablets to tell you the real truth, apart from the odd Panadol here and there for the good old headache.

I'd be lying like everyone else if I didn't admit that I have more stubborn mongrel in me than that of those Spanish bulls and the ferocity of that of a wild lion, but only if you do me serious harm; deep, deep, very deep down I am still just that little boy from Bolaro Avenue in Greystanes of Sydney, NSW who has a heart bigger than Phar Lap[23] and who gets serious and substantial joy from being able to help others in every which way that I can; I always just wanted to see those tears of sadness turn back into tears of solemn joy and slowly but surely fade and dry to a smile that simply couldn't be wiped off one's face.

---

23. Phar Lap was a champion thoroughbred racehorse whose achievements captured the Australian public's imagination during the early years of the Great Depression. Google. https://www.google.com/search?q=phar+lap&oq=Phar+Lap&aqs=chrome.0.0l6.1324j0j4&sourceid=chrome&ie=UTF-8 [Accessed: 12 May 2019]

Supercharged Goosebumps 2481

24 November 2018

After all the years of savage and chronic levels of abuse including from my own so-called father who I simply see as nothing but the ultimate coward, my deepest and honest opinion is that all these people who thrive on abuse, and equally neglect, are of the same pernicious nature and even more so are unbelievably and incredibly weak, pathetic and cowardly who only pick on people weaker than themselves. And from my many personal experiences of extremely high levels of emotional heartache, I just couldn't escape the reality of the sky-high anxiety eventually converting into depression.

The six main human contributors who were the most significant cause of most of my personal grief and misfortune and most definitely all of my emotional and psychological trauma are, in order: Frederick Stanley Smith; Rex Stanley Smith; Karen, who knows which surname but I like Justice; Wayne Lesley Earea and Gregory Earea; and none other than the infamous Dr Haritha Devineni.

But I just continue to laugh, sometimes uncontrollably, as to how piss weak they all are, and the fact that they all had to take all of their many personal woes out on someone like me, who clearly they all obviously saw as an easy target on many different occasions. Their incredibly weak and soft levels of personal character wouldn't and couldn't allow them to deal with personal grief situations in not only a civil manner, but equally an adult manner. Most of them used extremely high levels of alcohol and meted out even higher levels of physical, mental and emotional abuse to make themselves somehow feel an imitational sense of power and justice in some weird and wonderful way.

During the many, many phone calls and very deep face-to-face conversations with my lifelong great mate Simon Curtis over the years he absolutely agreed 100% they were all weak, soft and pathetic, just like an incredibly soggy wet tissue – I mean after all, he wanted to beat the shit out my father from age 16, as he hated and completely detested his smart-arse attitude and he despised him for calling him Simone instead of his real birth name, but this was Rex Smith's way of getting under people's skin, and I guess that was saying something as his father, Simon's I mean, was such an incredibly strong character who has sadly passed.

Good old Jim Curtis had shown absolutely no signs of personal weakness, in fact he reminded me a lot of myself, he said it how it was and wasn't afraid of doing so and neither was I, but being crucified for it was simply wrong. I always find it amazing how the victim in severe forms of bullying in nearly all cases through self-defence ends up being the perpetrator and this is wrong, but it is always through the manipulation of lies and deceit and there is just no arguing or denying that, and this sadly will never change when you are outnumbered by the abusers yourself which, in fact, the victim always is, you are quite simply fucked.

27 November 2018

I must make mention that on the night of the 14th March 2017 when we were celebrating my youngest's 10th birthday at a local Gold Coast surf club, Wayne Earea was spared his life. When I heard the sound of that distinct cleft palate of the little weedy boy-like man himself, I felt waves of emotional rage come racing from my feet all the way up my body like I had never felt before; that girly sounding voice sent my whole body into a shaking torrent of sheer adrenaline as all I wanted to do was pick him up and throw him over from some three or four stories high, my arms were rattling with fully loaded levels of adrenaline on the table as were my legs underneath, but thankfully my children's gran was there to calm my rage, she talked me around and provided me with a significant sense of calm. And surprise, surprise, Wayne Earea was as drunk as a skunk just as he had been some 30 years earlier when he had unleashed all the savage, chronic and seriously vicious and aggressive levels of abuse and rage towards me as a 16-year-old kid. He was incredibly lucky that night because if I had have been on my own he would undoubtedly have been thrown some four stories over, and I guess in turn so was I, as I would have been charged and imprisoned for the murder of a parasite.

26 December 2018

Somehow in some weird, wonderful and strange way although I'm definitely not grateful one little bit for all the constant abuse and, as importantly, the parental neglect since the age of 6 ½ years, but I would say that I am now content with what has played out over the many years; I do honestly have to be upfront and admit that without all the many extreme negatives and traumas that occurred when and how they did in my younger years of life, I simply wouldn't have coped with the ten years that I have had with my crushed foot and the crook leg itself. The abuse and equally the neglect so early in life forced me to battle, struggle and many times crawl, and also many, many times cry uncontrollably, but most of all it gave me the will to keep fighting and, most importantly, to try my utmost to stay strong, which at times has been somewhat tricky, but I simply wasn't going to stop, my personal DNA just wouldn't allow it. So, thank you to the many people who have had the opportunity to judge me, shit on me and kick me while I was down because you have all, quite simply, given me the high level of extreme inner mongrel to stay alive. What this life-changing injury with which I have battled since 25 October 2008, has done is given me an extremely significant level of resilience that is inexplicable and equally indescribable, but what I do know is I would happily step into the ring with Mike Tyson even with a crook leg, because in life it most certainly is not about how hard you can hit, but about how hard you can get hit and I have proven to myself and, just as importantly, to my three children, that I have indeed taken some of life's biggest king hits and I just keep getting back up, because you most certainly can't keep me down, my spring loaded character and my sheer mongrelness just won't allow it.

However, seeing countless families go through relentless and completely unwanted situations of grief to which they should never have been exposed, simply breaks and shatters my heart as well, including Charlotte Dawson,[24]

---

24. Charlotte Dawson was a New Zealand–Australian television personality who committed suicide in 2014. Google. https://www.google.com/search?safe=strict&ei=akfYXIerCqCn1fAP3PuW0Ag&q=charlotte+dawson&oq=charlot&gs_l=psy-ab.1.0.35i39j0i131l2j0i67j0l6.19930.22593..24394...1.0..3.149.1749.11j8......0....1..gws-wiz.....6..0i20i263j0i131i20i263j0i131i67.VwJosmKliAA [Accessed: 12 May 2019]

Jeremy Smith

Daniel Morcombe[25], Thomas and Stuart Kelly[26] and, one of Australia's latest devastating tragedies, the loss of the beautiful little Dolly Everett[27], and all the many women who have been interfered with and eventually murdered by public monstering predators sickens me to the core. Clearly, Australia has many problems in many different ways, but we weren't showing any serious sense of urgency in fixing and repairing the hundreds of problems within our justice system; all of those innocent victims should have still been alive today, but it is never going to be unless Australia tightens up its justice system with a sense of urgency and stops picking on innocent men like me. Not all men are monsters, but I certainly got treated like one by Dr Haritha Devineni and her female Indian counterparts, they ought to be completely ashamed of themselves, removed from all and every part of the Australian Medical Board of practitioners and shipped back to Mumbai.

---

25. Daniel James Morcombe was an Australian boy, aged 13, who was abducted on 7 December 2003. Wikipedia https://en.wikipedia.org/wiki/Murder_of_Daniel_Morcombe [Accessed: 12 May 2019]
26. Thomas Kelly died in a one punch attack, before his brother Stuart tragically killed himself years later. Starts at 60. https://startsat60.com/discover/news/stuart-kelly-thomas-kelly-parents-ralph-kathy-sydney-morning-herald-interview [Accessed: 12 May 2019]
27. Amy Jayne «Dolly" Everett was an Australian teenager who died by suicide after becoming the victim of cyberbullying. Wikipedia. https://en.wikipedia.org/wiki/Suicide_of_Dolly_Everett [Accessed: 12 May 2019]

21 January 2019

I must say with all the television that I was forced to watch, I was a huge fan of the Channel Nine Network and I was especially a massive fan of Georgie Gardner from the *Today Show* and I remember ever so very vividly late in 2018 when Georgie herself on air begged Australian men to stand up and help to defend their neighbours and their families from violent and abusive men in the domestic setting and within their local communities. Well I have to say Georgie, you are spot on and I agree with you 150%. Once upon a time I did protect some people just as a neighbour, which to me was always the appropriate course of action to take as far as I was concerned. Looking after the very soft, weak and vulnerable was and has always been my service and duty to the local community, but unfortunately for those mothers and children being abused and beaten daily by low-life cowards, like all the men withdrawing from the educational system because of the many false and misleading allegations and accusations about male schoolteachers and the actions taken against them, and as the deranged and delusional Karen Justice did to all types of men including me, I now sadly never get involved anymore in protecting people in public, nor neighbours next door or across the street being abused and beaten, because quite simply the ramifications just aren't worth the heartache anymore.

Jeremy Smith

To me it is purely a matter and issue for the police, and their hands are tied as well. But I have to say Georgie Gardner, that while I agree entirely with your thinking, thanks to the chronic abuse that Dr Haritha Devineni and her Indian female colleagues brought upon me with purely false and completely misleading allegations with no evidence to support these allegations against me, now there is absolutely no more help or protection from me whatsoever, everybody is on their own, which is incredibly sad but the circus clowns that are enforcing and legislating the rules and regulations have forced it to become this way, sad but very true.

I have always enjoyed studying the many different facets of Australian law as I find it not only intriguing, but incredibly invaluable on a personal level, especially earlier in life being self-employed since age 25 it did, in fact, save me a fortune in legal fees as well, but I must admit that I have never come across the particular avenue of law which legislates against extremely high levels of self-belief, confidence, self-esteem and most of all sharp, astute levels of competency and an extreme sense of urgency, maybe it was there in the notes, I possibly could have missed it but I am quietly confident that I didn't.

Just because you have achieved a university degree in something doesn't guarantee that you will be any good at what you have chosen to practise, and it most certainly doesn't mean you have high levels of intelligence – this was evident in many different departments of the Robina Hospital on Queensland's Gold Coast, especially in the mental health sector. And having your head stuck in many books for several years – and in a lot of cases up your own arse as well – the result of which you hopefully passed your final examination, doesn't give you permission or licence to be a pompous stuck-up arsehole, however, so many are and quite simply I couldn't cop it. Intelligence is gained by acquired life knowledge and indeed life's experiences that are thrown at every single one of us day after day, week after week.

I must say I have loved talking to everyone and anyone from barristers all the way through to toilet cleaners and treated every single one of them equally and with the utmost respect including the many homeless; I thoroughly enjoyed hearing all their many different and varying stories, and I genuinely cared and was happy to offer a helping hand.

One thing that I will never forget is the advice that was given to me by an extremely intelligent lady by the name of Wendy who, on several occasions, spent no less than 45 minutes per session with me in confidential phone calls at absolutely no cost to me and sincerely advised me to never go near a psychiatrist in my life ever again. She also seriously advised me that they are the most dangerous health professionals on the planet and I can honestly say

I am living proof of that. She continued to explain that this was because they all had so many extremely different views, opinions and delusional interpretations despite which they simply were never wrong. The sad part is though, that they all believe their own bullshit and in their warped, deranged and fruit loop minds they do in fact sincerely believe they know what is going on inside someone else's head and to all of you wondering actually what, how and why, do yourself a favour and do some reading and research on the Rosenhan Experiment[28] which explains it very clearly and very thoroughly in a nutshell.

Quite simply the psychologists are more in tune with people's mental health than the shrinks will ever be. All the shrinks were renowned for doing was writing up prescription after prescription which, in turn, was just masking the actual problem through what I call a Band-Aid solution of extremely heavy doses of sedatory medications. Any silly bastard could do that once they've studied mental health and, of course, the appropriate drug types and their properties, but the psychologists, especially the good ones, get to the bottom of it, which in most cases was simply the truth, something the majority of humans just can't stand hearing. Believe

---

28. The Rosenhan experiment or Thud experiment was an experiment conducted to determine the validity of psychiatric diagnosis. Wikipedia. https://en.wikipedia.org/wiki/Rosenhan_experiment [Accessed 12 May 2019]

me when I say Doctor Tayne Garforth most definitely made the psychiatrists look like complete fools, she absolutely knew about mental health and she was the real deal in my personal sessions with her just because of the very honest, open and very civil conversations.

When it came time for her to talk and share her professional advice to me, it completely blew me away, it was actually as though she was extracting everything from my mind and using her own voice instead of me using mine. She is an extremely intelligent human being, but it goes without saying, she is an ex-Western Australian policewoman who has seen and heard it all and used her combined life knowledge and training to help others. Tayne mentioned several times about how much her dad had taught her and what she had taken from it, I wish I could have said the same about mine, but all he taught me was how not to be at all like him; demoralising, humiliating, lacking in self-worth, high levels of negativity and pessimism, abusive and telling everyone and everybody closest to him that they were always wrong, wrong, wrong and wrong and that he was always right. Well, I am sorry to say Rex Stanley Smith, that you have been wrong your entire life and very rarely have you ever been right, and although I will never say that I have always been right, I have in the way that I have treated people unless, of course, they have tried to bury me which you did so many times. You will always be that unskilled failed developer, and even with your 35 years' service as a wine bottle dusterer who thrived on calling himself a manager, you still know absolutely nothing about money, that is the undeniable truth because you've got none.

What I will remember most about you though is how domestically violent you were, the chronic levels of abuse that you showed towards me and my mum and I will never forget it, in my world you were and still are the ultimate coward who got away with blue murder through volumes of manipulation and major control. But I would suggest and guess that being raised by someone who opened their legs to just about anyone together with a serial paedophile it goes without saying you turned out just the same, abusive, shallow and didn't give a shit about anyone but yourself and, for some weird reason, that deranged daughter of yours, but no doubt there is a story behind that as well, just as many have suggested to me.

12 February 2019

One thing that I will never, ever be able to forget about you is how over the years, for me no less than 40 years, you antagonised little innocent children, up to a maximum age of 9–10 years of age including my three, with my mum, your wife, screaming endlessly and begging you to stop, but you simply ignored the children's and my mum's agonising emotions and persisted with savage levels of torment and agony until those children broke and flooded into a tsunami of tears of heartbreak.

But what I have confirmed to myself about you was that you somehow needed that in the everyday part of your life for some weird, wonderful and troublesome reason for your own sense of empowerment, which was purely false, deranged and extremely delusional, and for me and many others, unbelievably and incredibly disturbing. Why my beautiful and loving mum ever stayed with you being the abusive pig that indeed you are, will always be beyond me and remain a kind of mystery to me. But we all know the real truth and the only reason is simply that of extreme levels of fear, and frankly that was wrong. I remember clearly the day when my eldest son Harry came home from a two day stayover at his nan and pops and had encountered a massive mental clash and locking of horns with his pop, and advised me that he had been locked in a bedroom for some 4–5 hours for back chatting his pop, Rex Stanley Smith. Only 2–3 weeks later Rex mentioned to me in conversation in front of my mum that my boy Harrison was, in fact, not a very nice human being. When I questioned him as to why, Rex proceeded to tell me that Harry had called him an arsehole and had told him to get fucked in a rage of teary emotions. I simply said to Rex, "That's fine, I have absolutely no problem with that whatsoever," as I went into a fit of laughter. "I told him to stand up to you Rex and quite simply you couldn't stand it, either you 100% dictate to only people weaker than you and if they didn't cooperate in full with your super control freak ways you did everything you could to crucify them accordingly." I also told Rex that I had told Harry that if it were to happen again, to sit pop on his arse, something I had seriously regretted my entire life not doing. I also informed my son Harry if it did happen again that I would go and flatten him myself, something I had wanted to do since I was eight years old. Very simply Rex, in the kindest of words, is purely an ignorant, arrogant smart-arse and completely outspoken fucking arsehole, and I guess the truth did hurt.

But I guess the real deal breaker for me was when Rex sat on my couch and proceeded to tell me that Jack – my youngest son who was only aged six – was going to end up big and fat just like his mum's mother, his gran, something I will never, ever forget until the day I die. These are the major traits and behavioural patterns of a serial narcissistic sociopath, is it any wonder he has no real friends? I apologise Rex on everybody's behalf including mine and most importantly my three children for being nowhere near as perfect as you. You have lived a life of incredibly false and misleading representation of that of a husband, a father, a pop and most of all a human being, you are and will always be the weakest example of a human being I personally have ever met and encountered in my life to date. It is absolutely apparent to me that you needed to be crushed and I would be very happy to be the person to completely and utterly crush and destroy you without one bit of physical harm like you did to me because, to be frank, all I would have to do is take one very serious inhalation of oxygen and I know I could knock you out with one big massive puff. To me you are and will always only be a cardboard cut-out of what a human being really stands for, at some stage the truth had to come out and I am sincerely, unbelievably and incredibly happy to be on the end of that truth and would be more than willing to sit and settle the matter with any supreme court judge or, probably more appropriately, in the federal High Court.

I've had the deranged bitch there and she only lasted if I recall correctly about 3 ½ minutes before she 'bunged on'[29] the panic attacks and the crocodile tears started to flow, and I suggest Rex that you would probably not even last that long purely because of your personal bullying and cowardly weak sense of character, you couldn't stand being told the cold hard truth.

---

29. Australian slang for 'pretended'.

Jeremy Smith

Being forced to remain the best part of 10 ½ years couch or bed bound and having to adjust in so many different ways with nothing else to do other than watch huge volumes of television changed things. I now enjoy plenty of reading and love researching almost everything and anything – something that for most of my life I had no real interest in as my sport and business mad mentality and my zest and drive to succeed in life wouldn't allow me to sit still and I was simply unstoppable.

I honestly believe it's more than fair to say that you don't have to be a TV celebrity, a sporting legend or a rock 'n' roll superstar and most definitely not a politician, to fall on seriously personal heartbreaking tough times, like so many of us have. Sadly all of us average Joes know that, but that is all we hear about in the media and very seldom do we ever hear of all the other poor buggers experiencing their own form of personal heartbreak, struggling with life day to day, week on week, year after year in exactly the same way as all the public celebrity superstars do, and personally it gives me the shits, and has left a bit of a fair old sour taste in not just mine, but many millions of other people's mouths as well.

14

I CAN SEE THE CHEQUERED FLAG

After having such an abhorrent childhood not really absorbing, comprehending or understanding in my life the so many wrongs separated by the so few rights, it took me until a life-changing accident at the age of 42 to fully understand and comprehend how seriously wrong my childhood had been and the extreme level of parental failure on especially my so-called father's behalf as my parent and guardian. As a very proud and happy father of three myself, all of my children have been cared for and protected by me personally better than any form of royalty, and my astute parenting manner would not allow it to be any other way. I would never let them down at all in a way like Rex did with me and my two sisters, especially in the extreme event of a crime so insidious as that of childhood sex abuse, in fact, no abuse whatsoever, full stop. I always acted accordingly and most definitely immediately and that was my lifelong promise to my three children. They all knew very clearly that I would happily go to prison for any of them to protect them properly as is my duty as their parent, they have also been told that by several retired Australian soldiers in public as well.

For every single real human being, not the so many fake, false and misleading ones, but the so many legitimate ones, the fragility of life and indeed the seriousness of what it means to always remain at the highest level of ultimate happiness is something I believe we all take for granted together equally with our physical and mental health, I know I certainly did. We are all pretty much guilty of never stopping for long enough to sit still for a period of time to actually take it all in 100% and I personally and honestly believe that is where so many of us go wrong, we aren't ensuring anywhere near enough that we look after Number One and this is seriously important. But as all of us are seriously aware, it's incredible how quickly the world is now racing, there's no time to waste and there is simply no denying that.

From me to anyone reading this story of mine, please never take crap from anyone or anybody especially your own biological family members, and especially when, in fact, they are so very wrong and soaked in denial and oceans full of guilt from failing to act to the appropriate authorities purely to protect the family's name, after all, the Smith family from Byron

Bay was certainly absolutely not worth protecting, and was nowhere near any form of royalty but believe me when I say Karen and Rex both thought they were pretty close. Whatever you do NEVER let them, your family I mean, turn everything back onto you like my family did to me. Even though I was a victim of so much heartache and abuse both physically and mentally, in some bizarre way the authorities allowed them to turn me from victim into perpetrator through masses of lies, manipulation and just downright deceit, but very sadly this was the behavioural pattern of not only narcissistic human beings, but indeed lifelong bullies and I fucking hated them.

Whatever you do most definitely do not change for anyone or anything, stay and stand firm, stay and remain incredibly strong and take a serious stance for what you stand for and most of all just be yourself and don't allow them to break you like they broke me. But I do believe that it's very important to take down the grubs that try their utmost to take you down when you're at the most vulnerable time in your life. And this most definitely includes any grubby government clown who chose to believe a package of lies, because to me they are only people too, they breathe the same air and shit the same colour, but no doubt their shit has absolutely no odour.

To me a badge means absolutely nothing unless, of course, somehow you're breaking the law, that is seriously a different story altogether, but of course that was something I had never done, and I seriously drummed that into my three children as well. You may upset a few people along the way by telling the truth, because honestly all the serial grubs just can't stand hearing it, but I still insisted on telling them and they despised me for it, that was for sure. I guess it's fair to say that if you are going to treat people like garbage or ill-treat an animal, expect to be promoted as garbage and equally at some stage be prepared to get bitten too.

16 February 2019

It's certainly bizarre how the world has changed and it most definitely is for the worse and isn't showing any significant signs of important change in any way, that is a no-brainer. I guess it's apparent that that has something to do with the so many incompetent circus clowns who are attempting to run the world and failing quite dismally, and that most certainly applies to our own backyard of Australia. There are many varied and incredibly strange and obscure things that for me personally stand out like balls on a Brahman bull in some weird and wonderful way. They include me being a 1971 model with all the trims, bells and whistles, just kidding when me and my mates said we had a fish flapping around in the bottom of a net or a butterfly that we transferred into the butterfly house; and when we spoke about 'on the line' or 'online' we were grabbing our towel and boardshorts from it to go surfing at the beach or there was a fish on the end of it.

Oh, and even though it has caused some critical and major trouble to so many worldwide, to me ice will always be something that will keep my drink cool, and live with my foot wrapped in it day to day and quite simply I wouldn't have survived this long without it, but mine was only frozen H_2O.

And to anyone from the 50s, 60s, 70s and the 80s, a 'gig' was a great night out with your best friends and mates to enjoy watching an all-time favourite band of choice. A 'tablet' was something we generally put in our mouth to get rid of a headache. The 'web' was owned by spiders not Bill Gates; a 'trailer' was something we used to take stuff to the dump and generally on the back of some vehicle's tow ball. A 'mouse' was something that loved to nibble cheese and sadly usually ended up in a trap. And finally this one; 'speed' was something I had been head over heels in love with since I was a two-year-old little boy, but not the one that's classed as a drug, the one that drove all the adrenaline through my veins like no other. That's all I was, I was just a plain old adrenaline junkie, nothing more, nothing less. But some pretty serious, false and misleading allegations have led me to tell you my story.

I guess in summary that people are only as good as the way in which they wear their hearts on their sleeves or not, and I most certainly wore mine with pride and happiness. That is the undeniable truth and I've said it how it was and certainly am not afraid of doing so. I believe that as long as you always tell the truth you most certainly can never be prosecuted for anything. So, I guess it's fair to say the three main medical conditions that I suffer from are, in order:

1. NO BULLSHIT DISEASE
2. BLACK AND WHITE SYNDROME
3. SSAD better known as STRAIGHT SHOOTER AFFECTIVE DISORDER

These are serious medical conditions that were converted and reinterpreted by Dr Haritha Devineni and her team into bipolar affective disorder. What a pack of pompous dickheads, I certainly look forward to my day in court with these collusive circus clowns and most certainly invite any form of reprisal; I seriously welcome that with open arms.

Dozens of people who know me on a very personal basis – and indeed, all incredibly intelligent human beings – all came to the same conclusion as I did; that I was in an extreme state of "panic" rather than "manic", but Dr Haritha Devineni and her expert medical team undoubtedly knew better than anyone and everyone because, of course, they were the elite.

15

THE LAST LAUGH

27 February 2019

Today, the 27th of February 2019, is my big day which will hopefully determine an incredibly positive outcome for me moving forward as far as being able to walk and more, or as importantly, have no or very little pain for that 25–30 metres. I must admit that I am unbelievably scared and my personal anxiety levels are through the roof as my 10 ½ year battle with this injured and troublesome leg hasn't been without major and significant heartache, but I must say being under the care of Dr Ben Forster and Dr Rick Steer for this peroneal tendon bypass surgery has somehow, like Dr Matthew Hope, provided me with a sense of not only reassurance, but also significant levels of calm and to me that is huge. I would be incredibly and extremely grateful to be able to walk some 150–250 metres completely unaided and I personally have every single finger and toe that I own crossed and so do a heap of my personal best friends and select family members as well, male and female.

28 February 2019

So, my final surgery is hopefully now complete and as I woke from the general all I was interested in was whether they had removed both peroneal tendons or not? Did I have that incision just below my patella where Dr Rick Steer had advised me from where and how they were going to steal my hamstring. When I discovered that my two surgeons and their entire medical team had managed to save not one, but both of my peroneal tendons I was completed elated and overwhelmed with joy and shed a few tears alone in my hospital bed. With their combined level of extreme intelligence equal to their knowledge and years of experience the pair of smart buggers had excised just under four inches of my peroneus longus and braided both the brevis and longus tendons into one. They quietly suggested to me that there was a high possibility of being able to walk in some 6–9 months hopefully without any aid or assistance, and as Dr Rick Steer announced this piece of good fortune and then left my bedside those tears of joy managed to stream again.

This to me was better than any Powerball or Oz Lotto win; finally things were looking up for me and, as the old saying goes, "Good things come to those who wait" and I truly believe that almost 11 years is more than long enough to remain waiting, and more so to try and remain extremely patient, not to mention keeping a hold on my sanity, and I was indescribably proud of that.

On the night of the 2nd March 2019 I would, for the first time in 10 ½ years, begin to sleep for more than 1–1 ½ hours at a time in partial sleep – which was only rest really, not sleep – and would not find myself up wandering around the house 4–5 times up to seven times per night seven days per week. On that Saturday night of the 2nd March 2019 I actually slept for a staggering 7 ½ hours straight without even one pitstop to the loo for a radiator fluid extraction. What an unbelievable and unexplainable, amazing feeling and experience that was as I woke at 7.40 a.m. on the morning of the 3rd of March 2019 in a state of disbelief. This, most definitely after a very long, hard, agonising and heartbreaking 10 ½ year-long mongrel battle to keep my head above water and to simply stay above ground, gave me sheer and ecstatic levels of joy and excitement together with happiness I will never quite be able to put into words, but I guess some would say I was probably just experiencing another manic episode. What I insist on though is that I will never be able to explain what agonising and excruciating levels of physical, psychological and, equally, emotional pain can do to the brain, but I guess we can just call this episode a joyous piece of poetry which was something I loved as well. But my journey and experiencing this for real is something that I would never wish upon anyone, even the so many that had shit on me and judged me and chose to treat me so cruelly. I guess, like many of us, all I was put here for on Planet Earth was to be tested and challenged at the most extreme and ultimately the highest levels but I just kept managing to bulldoze my way through every little bit of it and trying as hard as I possibly could to stay highly positive, and at times it was certainly tricky but shit didn't that thing called sleep play a major and significant role in that.

17 March 2019

Speaking with many different types of people in all and many varying ways and forms of industry and indeed just everyday life, human beings are exactly and completely no different to me; 100% still struggle to believe what I had been forced to endure and was put through by my incredibly dishonest extended family members along with the absolute incompetence of the infamous QLD mental health sector of the Robina Hospital on the Gold Coast, on the sheer basis of believing a pack of liars rather than me who, in fact, was telling the undeniable 100% truth which Rex Stanley Smith despised hearing because of his abusive and cowardly persona. But as all those people, including many certified real medical health professionals, shook their heads in disbelief, they knew it was nothing other than the absolute truth, just pure and simple honesty and I had lived my life by it. In my personal view all and any governments globally should be keeping true blue and fair dinkum men and real deal blokes like myself onside, but I firmly suggest that it was a little late for that; clearly these ludicrous idiots were getting it wrong every single day, 365 days a year.

However, over this last long and incredibly trying time of the past some five years since my living nightmare date of 15th December 2013 – which was an incredibly tricky and testing time of healing from my horrific and frightening major nervous breakdown – and my genuine hatred of women I must reveal that this was changed by the care I had from ladies such as nurses Kim, Melissa, Sarah, Bec, Jess and the beautiful and caring Shellan of the Mater Hospital in Brisbane of QLD. They, along with three other highly professional, competent and courteous ladies with whom I have had dealings with along the way of my tireless journey as well: Felia, Clare and Celeste, you all know exactly who you are and I would just love to say thank you for all your care, common decency and most of all your incredibly high levels of integrity. Most of all I sincerely thank you for your very valid example of what represents a real woman and even more so, all true versions of what a lady stands for and what a true lady represents; I wish the world was full of ladies identical to you. I also sincerely thank all and every single one of you from the deepest point of my restored broken heart and because of all of you beautiful and big-hearted ladies my faith in the female population of global society has been restored; and because of all of you true and real examples of genuine ladies, from this day moving forward I will be stopping roadside to help those many stranded women with their flat tyre and/or puncture who I know have absolutely no chance of cracking those wheel nuts, let alone lifting not one but two car wheels, not to mention jacking up and releasing the jack with the car's weight and the safety precautions that surround the entire task. It truly is amazing and heartfelt how great people can, indeed do, change the way we view others and I am back to feeling like the real me; I am back to feeling like I did on the 24th October 2008, the day before I crashed into O'Reilly's mountain on the 25th of October 2008, a day my children and I will never forget. Why, you ask? Quite simply lower levels of pain 24/7 and feeling very positive and, indeed, hopeful that I will walk more freely in some 7–9 months from now, and the real big one – which to me is massive – is that I can now actually sleep, something most human beings take for granted.

I guess now all that really mattered to me was that I was increasingly beginning to laugh more often, and my sincere and genuine happiness was growing stronger and stronger daily and I have my team of surgeons to thank for that. I always – even in times of heartache, tumbling and falling moments – thoroughly enjoyed life and ensured that I always had the last laugh, but the most important thing to me was at the pinnacle point of my things-to-do list – equally with going around Bathurst for a blast; for the first time since my youngest son was born I was actually going to be able to play with him properly and words just can't explain how important that was not just for me, but it was massive for Jack as well. My personal injury had impacted him in so many ways – indeed, the entire family, and my personal hurt mirrored Jack's hurt, after all he is the spit from my mouth, his entire persona is identical to mine.

18 March 2019

I must touch on and mention briefly that the authorities, especially in Queensland, insisted that mental health didn't discriminate whatsoever, however I passionately and sincerely disagree 100%. I was severely and chronically victimised, discriminated against and abused by Queensland mental health at the highest level and diagnosed with a very serious psychiatric condition that I simply didn't have, but one thing that I completely understand now at nearly 48 years of age is that I quite simply don't like being touched by strange men. It is more than fair to say that no one can change a person, that's for sure, but someone or something can be a person's reason to change. And those people who were my cause for change were Rex Stanley Smith, Karen 'no Joy' Justice and the infamous so-called 'doctor' Haritha Devineni while the 'something' was clearly so many different forms of abuse. I never want to see these three human beings ever again in my life except, of course, in the High Court in Australia's capital Canberra, where I will seek a fair and positive legal outcome which I prefer to refer to as "Devine Justice". These people unquestionably need to be prosecuted not only for the many and varied forms and levels of perjury but, more importantly, all their many false and misleading accusations and allegations. Many lawyers, ex-senior police officers and all my great, close and sincerely honest friends, together with my children, believe they should all do significant jail time and I personally couldn't agree more, lock them up and throw away the key.

28 March 2019

Moving on with life and definitely moving forward with the gear stick in "D" or with a manual in "first" which indeed was all that I drove, I make absolutely no apologies for now being the extremely proud owner of a fully titanium steel strength – like the Sydney Harbour Bridge – accelerator foot, better known to me and all my personal best mates as a "true blue leadfoot" which indeed it was with some intricate throttle cable problems better known now as the peroneal braided line or tendons of course.

   I am also 100% extremely proud to hold my head high and announce to the entire world that even through so many different levels of extremely deep heartache and personal collapse, implosion and explosion, in my almost 48 years to date, I have not and would never take to a 6 ½ year-old child with a cast iron fire stoke in a rage to the top and side of the skull. I have not and would never use extreme adult male force with my hand or, indeed, a weapon in the form of a cane to physically assault a 6 ½ year-old little boy who, quite frankly, at such a tender age was quite simply petrified of life. I have not and would never abuse or physically assault a 15–16-year-old child in any form of an apprenticeship – or indeed at any point in their life – who is just trying to acquire knowledge and seeking honesty and trust within a working industry of employment. I would treat him as a younger brother and guide him through life just as Doug did with me and helped me acquire and learn the best possible life skills together with as much knowledge as possible in the most positive way. But I do promise to continue to have my many, many episodes of mania caused by my love and ultimate passion for fast cars and motorcycles as I feed the throttle and inject those potent levels of high octane fuel into those engines but, more importantly, over and above my serious loves and passions in life, I will always say it exactly how it is and will never hold back from telling the ultimate of truths. And I promise to always remain hard and strong and simply stand firm to expose all and any grubs who desperately try their hardest to seek and destroy men including me. To these people, including those such as Haritha, Karen, and any of the other weak and pathetic idiots, I will do the same, mainly those who thrive on power at the extreme highest level. Oh, and about Rex; I will continue to laugh just as I am right now over how incredibly piss weak he is and I strongly advise that he should seriously consider a set of 'bolt-ons' purely to stamp his act of feminism, but I guess as he is now so soft anyway that he is well on his way to fulfilling the ultimate and appropriate traits and ways of a (not so) lovely, (not so) well-spoken lady, and there is no denying that.

I am sincerely grateful that I have absolutely no signs of

weakness and cowardice and even more I am at the highest level of gratefulness and appreciation that I don't have one cowardly bone in my body, and that indeed I treat people the way in which I would expect and like to be treated myself, with respect, and if you don't like that – respect I mean – I am more than happy to treat you like a piece of shit as well. I was more than extremely happy either way of course, I only ever gave as good as I got.

15 April 2019

Throughout my entire life I have loved so many different walks of life and thoroughly enjoyed many heartfelt moments which I received from helping many different human beings who were in severe need of help, mainly in traumatic situations or sometimes just plainly needed a bit of muscle as they were struggling with whatever the task at hand may have been. However, one thing I must say is what has always concerned me the most at the highest level, up until 42 years of age and the unforgettable date of 15 December 2013, for the life of me I could never understand for one second, let alone one minute, why people wanted to kill other people. But after my personal experience with Queensland mental health and also their orthopaedic division as well at the Robina Hospital, mostly

Jeremy Smith

with Dr Haritha Devineni's abusive and reckless methods of brutality on the basis of Karen 'no joy' Justice and Rex Stanley Smith's chapters and barrages of chronic, misleading, false allegations and the extremity of their dishonest pathologically lying personalities, I now 100% completely understand with the utmost of clarity why human beings insist on killing other human beings. I sincerely and strongly suggest that hundreds of people would love to see both six feet under with the addition of a steel cage over their MDF[30] boxes with rapid set concrete dropped on top of them, I know I most certainly do. I hated these two arseholes with the utmost of passion that words could never quite explain, and because of these types of low life grubs including Dr Devineni, my hypervigilance has been frozen at the most extreme level and I have all but become a recluse, and to be completely honest that's the way I prefer it, my overall outlook on humanity has indeed been significantly changed. To me dogs are way better than people could ever be and if you harm or upset them, they will bite your arm or leg off and that is fine by me.

    I most definitely have lived a life of serious rollercoasters of emotions that's for sure, thanks to the so many different versions of brutal and savage abuse with unimaginable and

---

30. Medium density fibreboard.

unlimited levels of chronic fear, though I have to admit that being locked in those cages and jail-like cells when I had done absolutely nothing wrong – however, everyone else had – I have to say that this was the pinnacle of the biggest loop-the-loop rollercoaster ride I had ever partaken in unwillingly thanks to the complete stripping of every single liberty that I had once owned.

I guess that now coming to a final conclusion and nearing the end, being punished, humiliated and left with another chronic form of illness simply from telling the truth – and yes, extreme, most of it I admit, but honestly nothing but the truth – and being abused and crucified for it will never ever sit real well with me that's for sure. To me power crazy human beings are nothing but worthless scum, especially Karen, Rex and Haritha; it's fair to say that the 80–20 principle applies here as well. Lying, ducking and weaving as all cowards do to simply get around the truth will only ever be classed as an absolute disgrace to me, but I must admit that the day my story is released and becomes a public document I'd love to be a fly on the wall in so many different places all at the same time – I do know that sadly this would not be possible. Maybe in life we should all be very careful and wary of who we play games with and more importantly who we choose to abuse, but I happily admit that all are the weakest examples of cowards that I had ever had anything to do with and one thing that was guaranteed was that I always had the last laugh, and yes, Haritha Devineni, I do only play to win and don't you ever forget it. One day if you are not locked within a cage environment yourself or perhaps a jail cell I'd like you to explain to me in articulate detail what it was that you actually achieved with me, as I have never taken one of your toxic forms of BPAD prescription drugs since I was released from your so-called care that I prefer to see as savage abuse. I'd dearly love you to prove to me what it was you actually achieved with your overuse – and equally – abuse of your Queensland government power because my suggestion to you would be absolutely nothing, but shit, you gave me the utmost sensational opportunity to write the most compelling version of my events, enabling me to write a story that is seriously the best thing I have ever put pen to paper to in my entire life and I sincerely thank you for that from the deepest depths of my heart.

15 May 2019

So rounding up now and finally bringing my story to its final end the greatest piece of advice that I can give is that if you or anyone that you know of is being abused and/or equally being neglected by your biological family, especially like I was up until 15 December 2013, simply get away from them, get them out of your life and never be dictated to by anyone ever again, especially if you weren't breaking any laws. Because after all, there is absolutely no price you can put on your quality of life and most definitely your level and value of happiness, to me that was a no-brainer and I was living proof of that. How will I remember Karen and Rex you may ask; purely as narcissistic abusers who 100% simply had to get their own way or watch out, based on their personally extreme high levels of selfishness. And, as importantly, Karen I will best remember as a serial family wrecker including mine, and Rex wholly and solely as the "Cover up king" of paedophilia. But crucially, these are two people who quite simply didn't know or understand how to mind their own business; the other thing I guess as well is that neither of them knew their arsehole from their elbow.

One thing though that I must point out to the entire population of Australia is that the three words in the English language that most stand out to me that I will never quite fully understand the meaning of and which have caused me the utmost significant heartache are in this order: "interpretation", "trust" and the big one, "jealousy", better known to Aussies as the good old Tall Poppy Syndrome and shit, didn't I know so many of them, and Karen and Rex were at the extreme top of the list here as well. Just as disturbing is that throughout my life a word that I have never heard leave either of their mouths is the word "sorry". I guess after all Australia is riddled with many "gunnas[31]" and very few actual doers; I most certainly was at the top of the list of doers, whatever I said I was going to do I did with and beyond an extreme level of due diligence and, equally, extreme effort and I've proved this over my lifetime in many more ways than one, although my life-changing injury definitely slowed me down in so many different and frustrating ways.

Another thing though that I would strongly advise against is that if you wanted to be tried, tested and challenged mentally, emotionally and somewhat physically as well at the most extreme level, be sure to be captured by the grasping claws of Dr Haritha Devineni and let me know how you get on please. Who would ever have imagined that this story would derive from a missing bottle of Wild Turkey, prescription medication and an accusation of a workplace affair to my wife with substantial validity, a young boy with a childhood dream which he wanted to bring to reality, an old man by the name of Rex Stanley Smith desperately trying to cover up the crime of childhood sex abuse carried out against his three children and a 37-year-old man having a life-changing permanent disability who is now 48 years of

---

31. Australian slang for those who talk rather than act.

age and didn't know how to stop fighting. Believe me when I say the dominoes just kept falling over one by one, 45 years' worth of them to be precise, I guess it's fair to say that the cat is out of the bag now.

I must say and have to sincerely and honestly admit that I wasn't at all one bit a fan of seeing human beings die in any way or form because to me life was so seriously precious to each and every one of us collectively, however, I believe that Australia's federal government seriously needs to consider the death penalty for our daily growing rate of crime. And, in this order, the federal government should seriously look at these specific criminal types: paedophiles, rapists and serial killers; the death penalty would certainly be one way of stopping them and to me it's the only way, locking them up and wasting a fortune to house them just doesn't make sense to me one little bit. I am fairly confident that this would most definitely cut our crime rate and/or levels by 40–50% overnight, to me there is no other answer.

I truly hope that I haven't bored you with my story, however I seriously believe we have to look at a solemn "Royal Commission" into psychiatry and indeed also into these power crazy, deluded and deranged psychiatrists one by one because they certainly are destroying so many people's lives unnecessarily and daily; they tried with me but dismally and desperately failed every which way. If you have experienced in some way what I have encountered, I would sincerely and genuinely love to hear from you at this address abusedbyqldmh@yahoo.com.au.

I certainly hope that my once-great neighbours Monica and Ravi, who were fantastic people, but are on Dr Haritha Devineni's team, aren't treating people the way she treated me and, no doubt, many hundreds and thousands more as well who were just too scared to speak out, because if they are, I would be simply gutted.

A very serious lesson that I instilled into my three children from a very early stage in their lives was that once they had reached my age of now almost 48 years young, if they had one sincere and honest friend in their adult life on whom they could rely and confide in, quite simply they had won. Well, I am extremely grateful because I have three: Frank, Gilly and Uncle Bill and to be brutally honest without any of them I wouldn't have lived and survived; these blokes are seriously the real deal and I will always love them all for the support that they provided to me through the toughest time of my life to date and I will never ever forget what they did for me.

One of my daughter's closest friends was made aware of what I had been put through and disclosed that after some fifteen years plus her dad had to resign from his job, because he just couldn't tolerate any more of the abuse that was being inflicted and dished out to human beings in these public mental health "no care" facilities. The abuse, he admitted, was horrific, and surprise, surprise he was a psychiatric nurse who just happened to be part of Dr Haritha Devineni's team.

Oh, and by the way, on the 22nd December 2018 my good mate "Clava" all but ripped his left foot off the bottom of his leg in a frightening water-skiing accident, so now we are equal in our latest planned 2020 motorcycle race, he can't change gears real well and I've got an awkward rear braker, so we are fairly evenly matched. And didn't he have some mood changes due to pain, because after all, I have never seen anyone in agony jumping for joy, including me and I have been putting up with it for eleven years; to me and so many it was a no-brainer, but good old Les once told me and I've never forgotten, "You can't put brains in statues" and isn't that a fact. I've just got one last thing to do and I'm going to bust my balls to do it and conquer it to the best of my ability and that is to go for a blast around Mount Panorama at Bathurst, NSW, Australia.

So, to everyone that has judged me over my life-changing injury one way or another, screw the whole fucking lot of you, because to me as human beings you have no moral values.

I sincerely hope if you have read my story that you have

taken something personally from it as I now completely 100% understand in full why I have always been such an incredibly emotional human being for most of my life since age 5–6 years. I have had the hairs over my entire body stand end to end so many times and in so many different and varying ways and, together with my true passion and love for fast cars and motorbikes, this is why I chose to call my book, "Supercharged Goosebumps 2481".

ODDS ON 17 BLACK.

www.ingramcontent.com/pod-product-compliance
Lightning Source LLC
Chambersburg PA
CBHW070740160426
43192CB00009B/1511